The Wounded Knee Massacre and the Sand Creek Massacre: The History and Legacy of the Two Most Notorious Indian Massacres

By Charles River Editors

Soldiers posing with the Hotchkiss guns used at Wounded Knee

About Charles River Editors

Charles River Editors provides superior editing and original writing services across the digital publishing industry, with the expertise to create digital content for publishers across a vast range of subject matter. In addition to providing original digital content for third party publishers, we also republish civilization's greatest literary works, bringing them to new generations of readers via ebooks.

[Sign up here to receive updates about free books as we publish them](), and visit [Our Kindle Author Page]() to browse today's free promotions and our most recently published Kindle titles.

Introduction

A picture of Cheyenne leader Black Kettle and some of his followers on September 28, 1864. The picture documents what Black Kettle thought was a peace council with Governor Evans and Colonel John Chivington. Wynkoop is kneeling on the left. White Antelope is first on the left in the middle row, and Black Kettle is third from left in the middle row.

The Sand Creek Massacre (November 29, 1864)

Sand Creek is a relatively small stream of water tributary to the Arkansas River in a dry, sparsely-populated cattle ranchland area of southeastern Colorado near the Kansas border, but at this otherwise unremarkable location on the Great Plains, one of the worst massacres ever perpetrated against Native Americans in 250 years of ongoing conflict took place.

On the morning of November 29, 1864, Colonel John Chivington led 700 militiamen in a surprise attack against Cheyenne leader Black Kettle's camp at Sand Creek. Chivington was a fire and brimstone Methodist minister who had publicly advocated indiscriminately killing Native American children because "nits makes lice." Warning his men ahead of battle, Chivington stated, "Damn any man who sympathizes with Indians! I have come to kill Indians and believe it is right and honorable to use any means under God's heaven to kill Indians!"

According to Cheyenne oral tradition and several surviving soldiers' accounts, as soon as Black Kettle saw Chivington's men coming, he raised an American flag on a pole and waved it back and forth calling out that his *Wutapai* band was not resisting. Ignoring his cries for mercy, the soldiers commenced firing, cutting down an estimated 70-200 Cheyenne, about two-thirds of whom were women and children. The Cheyenne claimed that soldiers shot babies in the head at point-blank range, raped Cheyenne women, and scalped dead warriors. The following morning, Army Lieutenant James Connor, who had refused to follow Chivington's orders, visited the scene of the massacre and reported, "In going over the battleground the next day I did not see a body of man, woman, or child but was scalped, and in many instances their bodies were mutilated in the most horrible manner - men, women, and children's privates cut out . . . I heard one man say he cut out a woman's private parts and had them for exhibition on a stick . . . I also heard of numerous instances in which men had cut out the private parts of females and stretched them over saddle-bows and wore them over their hats while riding in the ranks."

Black Kettle managed to escape the slaughter, only to be killed during George Custer's unprovoked attack at Washita River in 1868, but Cheyenne leader White Antelope was killed and his body was mutilated. According to historian Stan Hoig in *The Sand Creek Massacre*, "The body of White Antelope, lying solitarily in the creek bed, was a prime target. Besides scalping him the soldiers cut off his nose, ears, and testicles - the last for a tobacco pouch."

The results of the massacre were precisely what Colonel Chivington hoped to achieve. The Cheyenne, who were at this time allied with the Lakota and Arapaho, vowed to avenge the needless deaths of Black Kettle and his people. Early in 1865, a coalition of 1000 Cheyenne, Lakota Sioux, and Arapaho attacked several white ranches and a military post along the South Platte River Trail near Denver, capturing wagon-trains, confiscating livestock, and killing several hundred white settlers in the process. Staying one step ahead of the U.S. Army, they continued to raid the North Platte Trail that summer, completely wiping out an Army wagon-train and taking its horses and supplies. In response, the federal government dispatched General P. E. Connor and a force of 3,000 men with orders to ignore any overtures of peace or compliance from the marauders, and to "kill every male Indian over the age of 12."

Since this order was coming on the heels of the Civil War, the Army was still in some disarray, and the Cheyenne managed to elude Connor's forces and take safe refuge in their hunting grounds. They even mounted retaliatory raids on occasion. Ultimately, however, the end of the war made an increase in westward travel possible, as well as the construction of more railroads and forts. The Homestead Act of 1863 essentially sanctioned white settlement of the high Plains, and once white settlers flooded into Indian territories, it became incumbent on the U.S. military to protect them from hostile tribes.

The Wounded Knee Massacre and the Sand Creek Massacre analyzes one of the most controversial events of the 19th century. Along with pictures of important people, places, and events, you will learn about the Sand Creek Massacre like never before.

A mass grave for the dead at Wounded Knee

The Wounded Knee Massacre (December 29, 1890)

"General Nelson A. Miles who visited the scene of carnage, following a three day blizzard, estimated that around 300 snow shrouded forms were strewn over the countryside. He also discovered to his horror that helpless children and women with babes in their arms had been chased as far as two miles from the original scene of encounter and cut down without mercy by the troopers. ... Judging by the slaughter on the battlefield it was suggested that the soldiers simply went berserk. For who could explain such a merciless disregard for life? ... As I see it the battle was more or less a matter of spontaneous combustion, sparked by mutual distrust..." – Hugh McGinnis, 7th Cavalry

Among all the events in the strained relations between the U.S. government and Native Americans during the 19th century, the most notorious and defining one was what is today called the Wounded Knee Massacre. Technically, it was the last armed engagement between Sioux warriors and the U.S. military, and it marked the end of effective resistance by any Sioux bands, but what actually occurred is far more controversial.

In late December 1890, a group of roughly 350 Lakota Sioux led by Big Foot and Spotted Elk were escorted to the Wounded Knee Creek area and ordered to establish a camp there, but fearing another possible uprising despite the fact the band was comprised mostly of women, about 500 U.S. Army troops from the 7th Cavalry Regiment, led by Major Samuel M. Whitside, approached the Lakota encampment on the morning of December 29 with orders to disarm and escort the Native Americans to a railhead for transport to Omaha, Nebraska. Some of the men in the 7th Cavalry had also been part of the 7th Cavalry at Little Bighorn, so there could not have been a worse command to send on a mission that required interacting with the Lakota.

As the troopers entered the encampment, a shot rang out. It is unclear who fired, but regardless, the single shot triggered a fusillade from the Army troops. One of the Army soldiers, Captain Edward Godfrey, explained, "I know the men did not aim deliberately and they were greatly excited. I don't believe they saw their sights. They fired rapidly but it seemed to me only a few seconds till there was not a living thing before us; warriors, squaws, children, ponies, and dogs ... went down before that unaimed fire." The resulting assault would eventually kill most of the Native Americans, including both Big Foot and Spotted Elk. Approximately 30 U.S. Army soldiers were killed and about 40 were wounded, nearly all struck by friendly fire in the chaotic, close-quarters shooting. Of the Native American dead, most were killed outright, but the wounded were left on the frozen ground to perish during the frigid night. The following day, the frozen bodies – which had been stripped by the soldiers for souvenirs – were buried in mass grave.

The Wounded Knee Massacre had several outcomes. The soldiers who participated in the massacre were commended and awarded for their actions, with 20 of them receiving the nation's highest military award, the Congressional Medal of Honor, for action during the "battle." At the same time, Wounded Knee would grow to become a source of inspiration for a generation of Sioux people who came of age in the 1960s, and they sought to reestablish negotiations with the United States as a sovereign and independent nation. The American Indian Movement would engage in confrontational and at times violent resistance to perceived U.S. government oppression at Alcatraz, the Bureau of Indian Affairs building in Washington D.C., and later the town of Wounded Knee, South Dakota, and the Wounded Knee Massacre site.

The Wounded Knee Massacre and the Sand Creek Massacre comprehensively covers the background leading up to that infamous day, as well as accounts of what happened and the aftermath. Along with pictures of important people, places, and events, you will learn about Wounded Knee like you never have before.

The Wounded Knee Massacre and the Sand Creek Massacre: The History and Legacy of the Two Most Notorious Indian Massacres

About Charles River Editors

Introduction

The Sand Creek Massacre

    Chapter 1: Background

    Chapter 2: Prelude to Sand Creek

    Chapter 3: The Sand Creek Massacre

    Chapter 4: Investigations of the Massacre

    Chapter 5: Historical Consequence of the Massacre

    Bibliography

The Wounded Knee Massacre

    Chapter 1: The Great Sioux War of 1876-1877

    Chapter 2: The Ghost Dance

    Chapter 3: Sitting Bull and the Ghost Dance

    Chapter 4: Big Foot and the Stronghold

    Chapter 5: The Massacre

    Chapter 6: The Aftermath

    Bibliography

themselves as belonging to a single tribe.

By 1800, the Great Plains was a checkerboard of more than 30 known Native American societies speaking at least six distinct language families. Across the Canadian prairies and what would become the states of Montana, Minnesota, and the Dakotas were Algonquian-speaking Blackfoot, Gros Ventres, and Plains bands of Cree, Ojibwe, and Lakota and Dakota (Sioux). The Plains groups further south included the Kiowas, eastern Apache, and Shoshonean Comanche. The heartland of the Plains was dominated by Algonquian Arapaho, Cheyenne, and Caddoan Pawnee, with the Osage, Kansa/Kaw, Oto, and Caddoan Iowa on the periphery. Since the southern plains bordered groups in the U.S. Southwest, numerous groups like the Utes and Shoshones made frequent forays into the Plains to hunt, as did the Nez Perce, who were closer to the Pacific Northwest.

Given these regional arrangements, it comes as no surprise that early European explorers had a difficult time distinguishing one indigenous group from another, or that misidentification became the norm rather than the exception. This also makes it difficult for historians to determine precisely when whites came into contact with the Cheyenne; some believe it happened as early as the late 1600s. Specific reference to the Cheyenne did not appear in official documents until the early 18th century, when fur trader, explorer, and diarist Alexander Henry the Younger reported that he had traded with "Cheyenne . . . wearing dresses of Spanish manufacture after being visited by a Spanish boat loaded with goods." But many scholars believe French explorer Robert Cavelier de La Salle was probably referring to the Cheyenne in 1680 when he wrote of meeting a "band of Chaa Indians" in present-day Illinois. There were also various reports made by Mexican and French traders who wrote of regularly visiting groups of the Black Hills who "traded hides for metal arrowheads and sheet metal", and even earlier French reports referenced a group that lived between the Mississippi River and Mille Lacs Lake in present-day Minnesota that hunted bison and collected wild rice, which some historians believe were the Cheyenne.

Additionally, a subsequent account from around 1800 speaks of "the great Cheyenne sickness", likely a cholera epidemic, that struck down an entire tribe: "One warrior, a brave man . . . came walking along the camp circle during this time singing a war song. 'I cannot see the enemy who is killing us,' the man cried. 'When I see an enemy I cannot stay back, but I can't protect the people from this thing; they just fall and die.' He was singing and talking that way between times, and when he walked back to his own tipi the sickness struck him too, and he dropped as if he had been shot, dead."[1] The inference here is that European contact must have been the cause for the spread of cholera and numerous other foreign diseases among the indigenous population, making it likely the Cheyenne had contact with them before 1800.

Despite their initial anonymity, once the group was recognized, the Cheyenne quickly became one of the most well-known of the Plains tribes among white settlers, which wasn't exactly a

---

[1] Wilson, James. *The Earth Shall Weep*. Page 263.

The Sand Creek Massacre

Chapter 1: Background

Cheyenne: Stump Horn and family showing Horse Travois. Photo taken circa late 19th century.

    The Cheyenne and the Arapaho were closely allied Algonquian-speaking tribes. Originally, both were sedentary agriculturists living in what is now western Minnesota and eastern North Dakota, but at some point in the 18th century, they began moving out onto the Great Plains, as did a number of similar tribes after the acquisition of horses from the Spanish or from other Native Americans. Relying on horses, they took up a roving way of life based on hunting the enormous herds of plains buffalo.

    The Cheyenne were organized into 10 semi-autonomous bands, each having four chiefs. These forty band-chiefs, along with four principle chiefs, made up the council which met periodically to consider matters of importance for the tribe. Men of fighting age were also organized into five warrior societies such as the famous Dog Soldiers. The Arapaho were organized similarly, although with fewer bands and no paramount chiefs. Reliable tribal population numbers are hard to come by, but ethnographer James Mooney estimates that at their peak during the 1860s, before incurring heavy losses in warfare with the whites, the Cheyenne had about 4,000 people, with 1,000 being warriors. By that time, the Cheyenne had divided into northern and southern branches, although people in the two branches remained in touch with each other and thought of good thing for the tribe. By 1825, the Cheyenne way of life came under threat from the U. S. Government when it proposed a "friendship treaty" (which included the Lakota and other Plains groups) that would allow safe passage for westward-bound wagon-trains moving through "Indian Country." However, the wagon trail cut a path across Cheyenne and Sioux hunting grounds that essentially divided the buffalo into two separate herds, and several Plains Tribes were forced to split in half, dividing both the Cheyenne and Arapaho into "southern" and "northern" branches. But over the next three decades, the Cheyenne and other Plains groups would attempt to maintain friendly relations with the U. S. Government even as numerous conflicts between Native Americans and the U.S. army erupted all around them.

In 1851, General William S. Harney convened a meeting, calling the Cheyenne, Lakota (Sioux), Arapaho, Crow, Assiniboine, Mandan, Hidatsa, and Arikara nations to Fort Laramie to negotiate territorial and "right-of-way" issues through their territory. U.S. officials wanted the Plains groups to end intertribal warfare so as to facilitate Harney's goal of allowing settlers to pass through the region in safety. As a result, the general was ordered to obtain permission from the Native American leaders for settlers traveling through Indian lands en route to the Pacific. This became even more imperative when the California Gold Rush of 1849 attracted more people west in search of riches.

General Harney

The government solution was to assign each band a defined territory where they were to remain, but such types of negotiation were meaningless to many of the Native American groups, who failed to see the validity of a treaty that was made without the consensus of all the leaders of their bands. Nevertheless, on September 17, 1851, United States treaty commissioners and representatives of the Cheyenne, Lakota (Sioux), Arapaho, Crow, Assiniboine, Mandan, Hidatsa, and Arikara nations signed the Fort Laramie Treaty, guaranteeing safe passage to white settlers taking the Oregon Trail in return for monetary compensation in the amount of $50,000 per year for a period of 50 years.

A photo of Fort Laramie in the 1850s

According to the terms of the Treaty, vast territory encompassing the lands between the North Platte and Arkansas rivers and eastward from the Rocky Mountains to western Kansas (an area including present-day southeastern Wyoming, southwestern Nebraska, most of eastern Colorado, and the westernmost portions of Kansas) would be subject to construction of roads and forts within "Indian Territory."

However, even though the Native Americans consented to the creation of roads and even forts along the route, they did not consent to settlers encroaching on the lands marked for them. The treaty resulted in a brief period of relative peace and mutual prosperity, but regional stability was ultimately destroyed by the failure of U. S. authorities to honor the most important term of the agreement: preventing the settlers (which may have numbered up to 100,000) from entering the heart of Native American lands during the Pike's Peak Gold Rush from 1858-1861. Moreover, the Fort Laramie Treaty of 1851 was rendered largely meaningless because of the nomadic movements of various Native American bands who were unaware of the existence of the treaty and continued their traditional raids against other Native American bands.

In 1861, Colorado governor John Evans convinced two Southern Cheyenne "peace" chiefs, Black Kettle (*Moketarato*) and White Antelope (*Vó'kaa'e Ohvó' komaestse*), to sign an agreement that surrendered a large tract of hunting land near what was becoming the thriving settlement of Denver in present-day Colorado. White Antelope was a highly-vocal follower of the teachings of Sweet Medicine, who said that chiefs are to be peacemakers, and he saw it as his spiritual duty not to advocate violence or incite controversy in any form. However, most other Cheyenne chiefs rejected further intrusion by whites and refused to sign any new agreement.

Around the same time, the great Sioux uprising that took place in Minnesota in 1862 ,when the United States was engaged in the Civil War, sent shockwaves among whites through the rest of the West. In Colorado, there was some significant concern that the Native Americans there might follow the Sioux example, and agents of the Confederacy were actively stirring up discontent among Native Americans in parts of the Southwest. The Cherokee and other "Civilized Tribes" in Oklahoma were mostly fighting for the Confederacy, but the Cheyenne and the Arapaho remained peaceful, which would be somewhat ironic in hindsight given that it would have been a good time for an uprising since most of the regular Army troops stationed in the region had been withdrawn to go fight the Confederates.

One of the Cheyenne signatories of the Fort Wise Treaty was Black Kettle, the leader of the Wotap band. Black Kettle (Mo'ohtavetoo'o) was born sometime between 1803 and 1807. As a youthful warrior, he participated in battles with the Kiowa and Pawnees, the Cheyenne's traditional enemies on the Southern Plains. In 1854, he became one of the 40 Cheyenne chiefs when his band's old chief passed. Black Kettle, highly-versed in the arts of war, would become a leading Native American advocate of peace with the whites, but his efforts would prove tragically futile, and he would eventually lose his life in the warfare with them.

In March 1863, at the invitation of Indian agent Samuel G. Colley, a number of Cheyenne, Arapaho and other Plains Indian chiefs traveled to Washington, D.C. The purpose was to overawe them with the strength and numbers of the United States. They had a meeting with President Abraham Lincoln, who advised them to give up their hunting and take up farming. Lincoln told them that was the source of the white man's power. Some sources say that Black Kettle was a member of this delegation, but his most recent biographer says that he elected to stay home. Regardless, he certainly heard reports and was influenced by what he heard.

Black Kettle

Colorado was organized as a territory of the United States in February 1861 (and became a state in 1876), and the two most important white men in the early territory were the governor John Evans and the military leader, John M. Chivington. Both were highly ambitious men who looked at Colorado as a stepping stone to advancement within the political system.

John Evans was a wealthy Illinois medical doctor for whom the town of Evanston is named, and he was one of the founders of Northwestern University, which is located in Evanston. As an influential Republican politician and personal friend of Lincoln, he was appointed to be the new territory's second governor in March 1862, and despite lacking any previous experience in dealing with Native Americans, Evans in his dual roles as territorial chief executive and Indian Superintendent made a sincere effort at first to maintain peace with the Cheyenne, Arapahos and other Colorado groups. He tried to convince the Native Americans who had not signed the Treaty of Fort Wise to meet up and do so, but many refused to come to a council that Evans organized in the summer of 1863 and denounced the treaty as a swindle. These Native Americans thought the buffalo their lives depended on would last for a long time yet, so there was no need to sink as low as to have to live on a reservation and engage in tilling the soil, which they considered women's work and was something their people had not done for a great many generations. They certainly did not want to leave their prime hunting grounds on the Republican and Smoky Hill Rivers.

Evans

This failure notwithstanding, Evans concluded his annual report as Indian Superintendent to the Office of Indian Affairs in Washington in October 1863 on a hopeful note that he thought the Native Americans in Colorado were now "feeling better." What caused him to change his mind suddenly and begin to steer matters in another direction was information he received in November from a white man who had been living among the natives to the effect that the Sioux, Cheyenne, Northern Arapahos, Kiowas, Comanches, and Apaches had all met and were planning a unified campaign against the whites in the spring – once they had acquired the requisite weapons -- and that they would merely pretend to be peaceful in the meantime. The notion of this grand conspiracy supposedly planned over the winter of 1863-64 loomed large in the minds of those who would later defend Chivington's brutal surprise attack on the Cheyenne at Sand Creek.

John M. Chivington, another Midwesterner, came in 1860 with his family to Denver from the Kansas and Nebraska territories, where he had served as a Methodist minister. A man holding strong abolitionist views, when the Civil War broke out he was appointed a major of the 1st Colorado Volunteers and became known as the "Fighting Parson." In the spring of 1862, Chivington won substantial praise for himself and his men in fighting against the Confederates outside of Santa Fe and helping to save New Mexico for the Union. After he was turned down for a transfer east to serve in the Army of the Potomac (in large part because he had no professional military training), Chivington returned to Colorado to seek other opportunities that would bring him further fame and glory. Chivington's father, Isaac, had fought Native Americans at the Battle of Tippecanoe (1811) in Indiana, and he apparently wanted to follow in his father's footsteps.

Notwithstanding his evident sympathies for enslaved blacks in the South, Chivington was full of hatred towards Native Americans. In August 1864, shortly before Sand Creek, Chivington had given a rabid speech at a gathering in Denver that left no uncertainty about what he intended to do given the opportunity: "Kill and scalp all, big and little; nits make lice."

Chivington

William Byers, editor of the *Rocky Mountain News*, is another man who played a major role in Colorado's early history. Byers made his fledgling Denver newspaper a big booster of the gold rush and Colorado settlement, and it gave prominent coverage to Native American "depredations." An editorial on April 23, 1861, while advocating conciliation with the natives, warned its readers in a racist kind of way that was not atypical for the times, "A civilized and enlightened people can well afford to remember that the tribes by which we are surrounded are our inferiors physically, morally, mentally, and that the commission of what we call crimes, assumes with them the merit of bravery and manly action." Consequently, whites should be prepared so that the natives who committed "outrages" could be punished firmly.

In short, attitudes among white settlers in Colorado towards Native Americans ranged from the liberal and paternalistic to the outright racist and downright genocidal. However, none doubted that the natives represented the past and were destined to fade away with the buffalo, while whites were the present and future of civilization. On the other side, Native American attitudes towards the incoming white settlers were tolerant at first but increasingly angry as they found more and more of their lands taken from them and as the numbers of buffalo began to diminish at the hands of white hunters. Clearly, a clash of some sort was bound to happen at some point, and whether it would take a peaceful or violent course would depend upon the different human actors involved and on the particular historical circumstances.

Chapter 2: Prelude to Sand Creek

As fate would have it, the actual commencement of hostilities between whites and the Cheyenne seems to have arisen due to a minor incident in April 1864. As an interpreter recalled Chief Black Kettle describing it later at a negotiating council, "While a hunting party of their young men were proceeding north, in the neighborhood of the South Platte River, having found some loose stock belonging to white men, which they were taking to a ranch to deliver them up, they were suddenly confronted by a party of United States soldiers and ordered to deliver up their arms. A difficulty immediately ensued, which resulted in the killing and wounding of several on both sides."

These 40 cavalrymen under Lt. Clark Dunn had been sent out on a mission to look for stolen livestock while following up on a ranch hand's complaint, and they had orders to disarm the Native Americans "but to use every means to avoid a collision with them." Upon seeing some crossing the river with a herd of animals, the ranch hand who was with the soldiers as a guide thought these were the same Native Americans with some of his stolen stock. At least, that was the official white side of the story; contradictory cultural views on whether free-roaming animals such as cows and pigs could be considered anyone's property had complicated relations between natives and whites since colonial times, and things escalated after this fateful riverside skirmish. There had been no interpreter present who might have enabled the cavalrymen to understand the Indians. The Native Americans had initially approached the cavalrymen and shaken hands with them, but they could not get across what they were doing with the lost cattle.

Meanwhile, another Colorado cavalry detachment under Lt. George Eayre was out searching for cattle thought to have been stolen by Native Americans in the area of the Republican River. Eayre had been told by Chivington to kill all the Indians he came across. His men destroyed and looted two Cheyenne villages and then killed a Cheyenne peace chief, Lean Bear, who was hunting buffalo with his band and had approached the solders in a friendly manner. Indeed, Lean Bear was wearing the peace medal that he received from his trip to Washington.

Adding more fuel to the flames of war that began with a misunderstanding, cavalry under Major Jacob Downing, acting with Colonel Chivington's permission and encouragement, set out in the middle of May to punish the Native Americans further. After forcing a captured Cheyenne to show them the way, they found a Cheyenne camp at Cedar Bluffs some 60 miles north of the South Platte River and attacked it. This was a surprise attack on innocent people who were totally unaware of there being any troubles going on between them and the whites. In a sort of preview of the Sand Creek Massacre a few months later, the white soldiers killed 26 and wounded 30. No Native American prisoners were taken, and the village was plundered and burned to the ground. A pleased Downing later reported to Chivington, "I believe now it is but the commencement of war with this tribe, which must result in their extermination."

Downing

With the prevailing belief among whites of a Plains-wide Native American conspiracy as background, the news of a white family having been killed and scalped by natives on June 11, 1864 at their home on a ranch about 25 miles southeast of Denver came as a thunderbolt. This "Hungate Massacre," named after the murdered family, was apparently perpetrated by a rogue band of Arapahos who were out stealing livestock, and while their motivation for killing the Hungates remains unclear, it was possibly revenge for previous hard dealings from the absent ranch owner.

Regardless, the victims' horribly mutilated bodies were brought to Denver and displayed, whipping up violent anti-Indian hysteria, and Governor Evans now concluded that the full-scale Indian war that he and other whites had been anticipating was upon them. He telegraphed east for help – with battles raging between the Union and the Confederacy, none was available – and sent a dispatch to Col. Chivington commanding the 1st Regiment of Colorado Cavalry. Chivington, in turn, ordered his officers to proceed in force after the natives and not to "encumber" themselves with taking any prisoners.

What followed during the summer of 1864 was more or less open warfare with the Plains Indians. On July 24th, Governor Evans issued a proclamation to "the friendly Indians of the Plains" that declared, "The Great Father is angry [about depredations against livestock, soldiers and civilians by the Indians] . . . but he does not want to injure those who remain friendly . . . I direct that all friendly Indians keep away from those who are at war, and go to places of safety. Friendly Arapahoes and Cheyennes belonging on the Arkansas River will go to Major Colley, . . . at Fort Lyon, who will give them provisions and show them a place of safety." Not long after that, Evans called upon Colorado citizens to feel free to kill any natives whom they deemed hostile This was like declaring open season on them in Colorado, since those who killed natives were, by virtue of Evans's proclamation, entitled to keep their seized property.

During the summer of 1864, an additional regiment of cavalry was raised in Colorado for the purposes of protecting Denver and combating the Native Americans. This was the 3rd Colorado Cavalry Regiment, whose men were only volunteering to serve on an emergency basis for 100-days. Most of its citizen-soldiers had very little or no military training or battlefield experience.

For their part, Sioux, Cheyenne, Arapaho and other Plains Indian raiding parties attacked wagon trains and stage coaches on the overland trails. Travel on the Oregon Trail along the Platte River, which carried not only westbound human traffic but also considerable amounts of freight to supply the new western settlements and was the route stretched by the new cross-continental telegraph line, was effectively severed for over a month. At the same time, Denver was cut off in communications with the rest of the country.

Among the Cheyenne, the militant Dog Soldiers were often found in the forefront of the attacks against the whites. The chiefs, older and wiser men, complained that they had lost control over the young hot-headed warriors. However, when Arapaho chief Left Hand tried to demonstrate his peaceful intentions by coming with some warriors to Fort Larned in western Kansas, near where they were camped to offer their help in catching and returning livestock that had been taken by the Kiowas (traditional enemies of the Cheyenne and the Arapaho), they were shot at by the soldiers.

At the urging of William Bent, who ran a trading post called "Bent's Fort" on the Arkansas River and was married to the daughter of a Cheyenne chief, some Southern Cheyenne led by Black Kettle decided to accept Governor Evans' offer. Although Black Kettle thought the whites were the aggressors, he was concerned about the welfare of his people, so he and a number of chiefs signed two letters dated August 29th proposing a parley that would start by making an exchange of prisoners. These letters were taken to the closest military post, Fort Lyon, by a chief who had lived among the whites and could speak some English.

This led to a productive encounter on September 10th on a branch of the Smoky Hill River near the Kansas border, involving a large body of 2000 Indians encamped there and a 125-man detachment of cavalry from the 1st Regiment of Colorado Volunteers under Major Edward W. Wynkoop, the commander of Ft. Lyon. Wynkoop acted on his own initiative, explaining later that freeing the white prisoners had been at that time his primary concern. At the parley, after some early tense moments in which several Indian chiefs spoke out passionately about injuries they had suffered at the hands of the whites – one chief related how his brother had been shot and killed by soldiers when he had tried to speak with them about how he wanted to live peacefully with whites – they all said they wished to remain friendly and would let bygones be bygones.

Wynkoop

Black Kettle, as the principal chief of the southern branch of the Cheyenne, had the final word among the chiefs sitting in council with the white soldiers. He reminded them that the Cheyenne and the Arapaho, who could easily have attacked the whites when they first came into their territories, had always tried to be friendly to the whites and adhere to the terms of their treaty. He thought there were both bad natives and bad white men who were the ones causing all the trouble, but he believed their troubles would be over if they all followed the advice of the "tall chief," Major Wynkoop. Wynkoop told the chiefs that he was not a big enough official to make peace with them himself, but he could invite them to accompany him to Denver for a meeting with the men who could do so, and he would guarantee their safety. He also suggested that the other natives move closer to the fort.

After this round of conferring, Wynkoop removed his men at the chiefs' request to avoid any trouble with the young braves, bringing them to a camp some miles closer to Ft. Lyon. A day or two more were required, but the Cheyenne and Arapaho managed to locate and bring in four white captives, including a girl and three young children. Three of these captives had been taken at the Little Blue River in Nebraska earlier in August 1864 and had been traded by the Sioux to the Arapaho Chief Left Hand at the Smoky River camp. The balance of the seven promised captives had not been located, but the natives said they would continue to look for them and would buy them from the Sioux if necessary. At the same time, the natives thought some of their people were being held captive in Denver, but Wynkoop informed them that there were none held there.

As a result of the talks at Smoky Hill River, Black Kettle, White Antelope, and some others of the older, more peacefully-inclined Cheyenne and Arapaho chiefs - seven chiefs altogether – were able to accompany Major Wynkoop to Camp Weld in Denver. There, on September 28th, the group met with Governor Evans and Colonel Chivington and even sat for the taking of an official photograph. To show their sincerity, the chiefs offered to help in getting other tribes to make peace and to fight any hostile natives on the side of the whites.

Members of the Native American delegation in Denver

From that Denver meeting, the Cheyenne and Arapaho chiefs who attended left with the belief that things were now all right and deemed that the matter was settled. In fact, Black Kettle hugged Governor Evans and Major Wynkoop, and hands were shaken all around. The native leaders unquestionably told their people the same thing upon returning to the camp, which meant the tribes could now focus their energies on getting ready for the upcoming winter months. However, Evans had not told them exactly that; what he told them is that he had tried to make peace with them the previous year, but they had rejected his offer at that time. Thus, he could no longer make peace with them now since they were currently at war, which meant the disposition of the natives was to be left in the hands of the military authorities. In effect, Evans washed his hands of a touchy political situation; he probably did not want be in the position of being seen by other Colorado whites who were greatly incensed at the Indian "depredations" as giving in to any of them. Cutting his ties even further, in a letter to the Indians' agent, he said that the natives would no longer have to be cared for.

Colonel Chivington, who had said relatively little at the meeting except for bragging about his prowess as an Indian fighter, seemingly concurred. On that basis, Wynkoop extended to the chiefs the assurance that they would be protected under him. As a result, natives began to come in to Fort Lyon until there were 400 Cheyenne and Arapaho camping at the post. Wynkoop issued them half-rations, and everything seemed to be going very well.

Around this time, Governor Evans left on a trip to conduct treaty talks with the Utes in his capacity as Colorado Indian Commissioner, after which he traveled to the East. With Evans gone, Colonel Chivington was the main man on the scene left to deal with the Cheyenne and Arapaho, and he was spoiling for a fight. His 3rd Cavalry Regiment had seen little action against the natives and had acquired the scornful nickname of the "Bloodless Third," and Chivington complained to headquarters about what he felt was Wynkoop's overly conciliatory attitude towards the natives. As a result, Major Wynkoop was removed from command of Fort Lyon and replaced by Major Scott Anthony, who favored a more aggressive policy like Chivington. Anthony had been in charge of Fort Larned in Kansas when it had come under attack, and he had attacked some of the same natives whose chiefs were in Denver trying to make peace.

Anthony

Upon taking command of Fort Lyon on November 2, Anthony decided to treat the many

Indians who had gathered around the fort since October as prisoners-of-war, and he issued them some meager prisoner rations. When asked, the natives said they were fine with being treated in that way, but after 15 days, to the dismay of the natives, Anthony informed them that he would no longer issue them rations and that they should go out to hunt buffalo. To enable them to do that, he returned their weapons to them that had been previously confiscated. Moreover, Anthony told them that he had no authorization to offer them peace. Having heard nothing back from his superior officer, Major General Curtis in Kansas, it seems Anthony had become afraid of being attacked at the fort.

In suggesting that they vacate the vicinity, Anthony told the natives to go out and camp at Sand Creek and await word from departmental headquarters, which, when it came, he would relay to them there. Although they were not happy with his new arrangement and spoke scornfully of Major Anthony among themselves as "Red-Eyes" (he was recovering from scurvy), this is what the Cheyenne under Black Kettle did, as did some of the Arapaho, while most of the Arapaho under Little Raven went to a camp sixty miles lower down on the Arkansas River. Nevertheless, natives kept coming back to the fort, and, just three days before the massacre, Black Kettle appeared at the fort and was given a tobacco pouch by Anthony and the Indian agent for the Cheyenne and Arapahos, Samuel G. Colley, for the maintenance of the peace.

Sand Creek was about 35 miles away across the open prairies from Fort Lyon, and the native camp site was above the creek at a location used previously by Indians through the centuries in part because it had a good spring. Typically, Sand Creek is practically dry in November, making the spring vital. The Cheyenne encampment included 100 or more lodges, while an Arapaho encampment under Chief Left Hand that was located somewhat apart had eight or ten lodges. According to maps of the location of the massacre made by several contemporaries and recent spatial assessments made by archaeologists based on the locations of recovered artifacts, the Cheyenne encampment covered up to half a mile along the creek bank. Based on the numbers of lodges in the camp with an average of five or six occupants per lodge, the encampment's total human population was probably around 500 (although Chivington would estimate much larger numbers to inflate his "success"). About 200 were male warriors, while the rest were women and children.

Ethnographer George Bird Grinnell, who spent many years living with the Cheyenne and wrote about them extensively (his *The Cheyenne Indians: Their History and Ways of Life* is still in print), spoke with survivors of the Sand Creek Massacre at the end of the 19th century. According to them, Major Anthony intentionally misled the natives into staying at Sand Creek so they would be within range of a future cavalry attack. Whether this is true or not, the attack on the unsuspecting group was not long in coming.

Chapter 3: The Sand Creek Massacre

"My shame is as big as the earth…I once thought that I was the only man that persevered to be the friend of the white man, but it is hard for me to believe the white man anymore." – Black Kettle

While the Cheyenne and Arapaho chiefs met in Denver on September 28, 1864 and left in the strong belief that they had secured protection for their people, Major General Samuel R. Curtis, the head of federal forces west of the Mississippi, had telegraphed Colonel Chivington: "I want no peace till the Indians suffer more…No peace must be made without my directions." Chivington claimed later that Indian agent Samuel E. Colley had told him he had been able to do nothing with the natives for the past six months and that, in his opinion, they should be punished for their hostile acts. Colley later denied he said that.

Curtis

In his telegram, Major General Curtis did not call for an indiscriminate attack on Native Americans; in fact, he distinguished between good ones and bad ones, specifically citing

Arapaho Chief Left Hand as belonging to the former category. This was a distinction that would be ignored by Chivington, who was spoiling for a fight regardless of which natives he encountered. Keeping his movements secret -- even Evans was left out of the loop – and letting his officers and men think they were going off to fight hostile natives, Chivington moved his troops 260 miles in less than six days through cold weather and heavy snow to reach Fort Lyon on the morning of November 28, 1864. The troops under his command consisted of the 3rd Regiment of Colorado Volunteers, under the immediate command of Colonel George L. Shoup (later the first governor of Idaho), and the 1st Battalion from the 1st Regiment of Colorado Volunteers.

Shoup

Upon arriving at Fort Lyon, Chivington threw up his own picket around the fort to prevent any leakage of information despite having no military authority there. Fort Lyon, although located in Colorado Territory, was a part of the Arkansas military district and thus not under Colonel Chivington's jurisdiction since he was in command of the Colorado military district. When some of the officers who were stationed at the fort tried to explain to Chivington the existing arrangement with the natives camped at Sand Creek and their peaceful character, Chivington vociferously damned anybody who would have sympathy with them. Lt. Joseph D. Cramer, who would later provide some of the most damning testimony against Chivington, claimed Chivington shook his fist at Cramer and told him "he had come to kill Indians, and believed it to be honorable to kill Indians under any and all circumstances."

Major Anthony, although initially surprised at Chivington's sudden arrival, was easily persuaded to go out after the Native Americans. In fact, he claimed he would have fought them before but lacked a sufficient force to do so. From the soldiers stationed at the fort, Anthony contributed men for the punitive expedition from the 1st Regiment's 2nd Battalion, making the total number come to around 750. To those of his subordinates who questioned him about going after the peaceful natives at Sand Creek, Anthony suggested that they would deal with any bad ones there and save good ones like Black Kettle. After that, they would go on to attack the bad ones encamped at Smoky River. A piece of evidence indicating that this was not a totally disingenuous statement on Anthony's part is that he ordered the issuance of rations to his men lasting for a long expedition of 23 days away from Ft. Lyon.

In terms of armaments, along with the usual assortment of rifles, carbines, side-arms and sabers carried by western cavalrymen, the militia brought four mountain howitzers (two contributed by Anthony from the fort), which were smaller versions of the cannons used elsewhere by both sides in the Civil War. These howitzers could fire 12-pound solid and explosive shot with devastating effect.

Overnight, the combined forces marched for eight hours some 40 miles across the prairies from Fort Lyon to Sand Creek, guided by a fur trapper and a native "half-breed." As a result, the attack occurred in the dawn just before sunrise the next morning, November 29, 1864. The approaching troops were spotted by an early-rising native woman and initially mistaken for a herd of buffalo. To make sure there was no mistake about their identity, Black Kettle is said to have put an American flag he had been given, as well as a white flag, on a tall lodge pole next to his lodge. Some of the natives gathered there for their chief's protection, but that turned out to be of no avail. According to Robert Bent, an American guide, "I saw the American flag waving and heard Black Kettle tell the Indians to stand around the flag, and there they were huddled — men, women, and children. I also saw a white flag raised. These flags were in so conspicuous a position that they must have been seen. When the troops fired, the Indians ran, some of the men into their lodges, probably to get their arms… I think there were 600 Indians in all. I think there were 35 braves and some old men, about 60 in all… the rest of the men were away from camp, hunting…"

A white trader, John S. Smith, who was staying at Sand Creek with his Cheyenne wife, went out to try to ascertain the intentions of the soldiers. Instead of being provided with any explanation, he was shot at. Smith later testified, "I was in the camp of the Cheyennes when Chivington made his attack…I was, at the time of the attack, sleeping in a lodge…I could see the soldiers begin to dismount. I thought they were artillerymen and were about to shell the camp (Chivington brought 4 12lb canons to Sand Creek-It was the only time in Colorado history canons were used in any type of fighting conflict)…I went to the northeast, I ran about five miles, when I came across an Indian woman driving a herd of ponies…she was a cousin of mine- one of White Antelope's daughters. I went with her to the Smoky Hill (river). I saw as soon as the firing began, from the number of troops, that there could be no resistance, and I escaped..."

As terrified natives scrambled out of their teepees and tried to figure out what was going on, the cavalry troops launched their attack on the encampment, with some of them approaching overland while others approached via the mostly-dry stream bed. Most of the cavalrymen would fight the battle dismounted, but the assault on the camp was begun by a battalion charging and quickly separating the natives from their large herd of riding animals, making it harder for them to fight back or to flee from the scene.

Robert Lindneaux's depiction of the attack

As they were trained to do from boyhood, Cheyenne and Arapaho warriors tried to defend their people. Upstream from the camp, they hastily dug shallow trenches in the sand of the creek's bed or walls, and as women and children fled northward up the bed of the creek, they used that slight protection to fire back at the cavalrymen and occasionally run out against the soldiers on suicidal charges. However, the cavalrymen had the advantage of higher ground on the banks of the creek, and they brought several of their howitzers to fire explosive shells at the natives. The fighting raged for hours several miles along the creek bed, and each time that the natives fell back and retrenched, the white soldiers followed them along the banks.

The shooting in and around camp went on for as long as seven hours, and when the fighting was over, trenches were found piled full of the bodies of warriors who had sacrificed their lives to save their families and friends, many of whom were able to get away from the awful mêlée to a place of safety elsewhere. Even Major Anthony, certainly no friend of the natives, later remarked favorably upon the warriors' great bravery.

Of course, the fact that many escaped didn't mean the cavalrymen let them go. Fleeing natives were pursued for miles, with many run down and killed by the cavalrymen. At least 150 natives lay dead, along with eight cavalrymen, and no prisoners were taken. Indeed, several who had tried to surrender were shot. Major Anthony himself recalled, "There was one little child, probably three years old, just big-enough to walk through the sand. The Indians had gone ahead, and this little child was behind, following after them. The little fellow was perfectly naked, traveling in the sand. I saw one man get off his horse at a distance of about seventy-five yards and draw up his rifle and fire. He missed the child. Another man came up and said, let me try the son of a b-. I can hit him.' lie got down off his horse, kneeled down, and fired at the little child, but he missed him. A third man came up, and made a similar remark, and fired, and the little fellow dropped."

When the fighting was over, the bodies of the dead were scalped and mutilated. Most of the scalping and mutilation of Indian bodies seems to have been done by the poorly-trained 100-day men in the 3rd Colorado Cavalry Regiment, but it's apparent that other men participated as well. A junior officer testified to one of the official investigations about what he had seen after the fighting was all over (and which had left him totally disgusted): "In going over the battle-ground the next day I did not see a body of man, woman, or child but was scalped, and in many instances their bodies were mutilated in the most horrible manner—men, women, and children's privates cut out, &c ; I heard one man say that be had cut out a woman's private parts and had them for exhibition on a stick ; I heard another man say that he had cut the fingers off an Indian to get the rings on the hand; according to the best of my knowledge and belief these atrocities that were committed were with knowledge of J. M. Chivington, and I do not know of his taking any measures to prevent them ; I heard of one instance of a child a few months old being thrown in the feed-box of a wagon, and after being carried some distance left on the ground to perish ; I also heard of numerous instances in which men had cut out the private parts of females and stretched them over the saddle-bows, and wore them over their hats while riding in the ranks. All these matters were a subject of general conversation, and could not help being known by Colonel J. M. Chivington."

Similarly, one American guard, Robert Bent, described the scene: "After the firing the warriors put the squaws and children together, and surrounded them to protect them. I saw five squaws under a bank for shelter. When troops came up to them they ran out and showed their persons, to let the soldiers know they were squaws and begged for mercy, but the soldiers shot them all…. There were some thirty or forty squaws collected in a hole for protection; they sent out a little girl about six years old with a white flag on a stick; she had not proceeded but a few steps when she was shot and killed. All the squaws in that hole were afterwards killed, and four or five bucks outside. The squaws offered no resistance. Every one I saw dead was scalped. I saw one squaw cut open with an unborn child, as I thought, lying by her side. Captain Soule afterwards told me that such was the fact...I saw quite a number of infants in arms killed with their mothers."

As if the human toll wasn't enough, the camp's teepees were put to the torch, and any possessions left behind by the natives, including supplies of flour, sugar, coffee and tea, were heaped onto huge piles and burned. Horses that should have been turned over to the government were divided up among the soldiers to be taken home or sold as plunder. Recent systematic searches of the battlefield using metal detectors have turned up a wide array of items like cooking pots, tin cups and plates, and coffee grinders and pots abandoned by owners as they fled from the scene, and while some defenders of the attack claimed afterwards that articles found by soldiers had originally come from white wagon trains or white settlements, a more likely explanation is that any such goods were ones received by natives as part of their annuity promised by the two treaties they had signed in exchange for giving up their lands.

The Arapaho Chief, Left Hand, was shot to death early in the attack; he had stood with his arms folded announcing he would not fight the white men because they were his friends. According to Lt. Joseph Cramer after the massacre, "Black Kettle said when he saw us coming, that he was glad, for it was Major Wynkoop coming to make peace. Left Hand stood with his hands folded across his breast, until he was shot saying, 'Soldiers no hurt me – soldiers my friends.'"

Cheyenne chiefs killed at Sand Creek included White Antelope, One Eye, War Bonnet, Standing Water, Spotted Crow, Two Thighs, Bear Man, Yellow Shield, and Yellow Wolf. Ironically, One Eye had been acting as a spy for Major Wynkoop at the time. One white man on hand recalled, "On the day of the attack. He asked me many questions about the chiefs who were there, and if I could recognize them if I saw them. I told him it was possible I might recollect the principal chiefs. They were terribly mutilated, lying there in the water and sand; most of them in the bed of the creek, dead and dying, making many struggles. They were so badly mutilated and covered with sand and water that it was very hard for me to tell one from another. However, I recognized some of them – among them the chief One Eye, who was employed by our government at $125 a month and rations to remain in the village as a spy. There was another called War Bonnet, who was here two years ago with me. There was another by the name of Standing-in-the-Water, and I supposed Black Kettle was among them, but it was not Black Kettle. There was one there of his size and dimensions in every way, but so tremendously mutilated that I was mistaken in him. I went out with Lieutenant Colonel Bowen, to see how many I could recognize."

In fact, Black Kettle and his severely-injured wife, Medicine Woman, had somehow survived, and with other Sand Creek refugees, they were able to reach the safety of the Cheyenne Smoky

Hill encampment. A few natives stayed nearby to observe from a hill but then left when the cavalry remained in the village. One of the survivors remembered, "Everyone was crying, even the warriors and the women and children...Nearly everyone present had lost some relations or friends, and many of them in their grief were gushing themselves with their knives until the blood flowed in streams."

Adding to the horror, when the cavalrymen noticed one injured native still alive the following day, they summarily executed him. According to Corporal Amos C. Miksch, "Next morning after the battle, I saw a little boy covered up among the Indians in a trench, still alive. I saw a major in the 3rd regiment take out his pistol and blow off the top of his head. I saw men unjointing fingers to get rings off, and cutting off ears to get silver ornaments. I saw a party with the same major take up bodies that had been buried in the night to scalp them and take off ornaments. I saw a squaw with her head smashed in before she was killed. Next morning, after they were dead and stiff, these men pulled out the bodies of the squaws and pulled them open in an indecent manner. I heard men say they had cut out privates, but did not see it myself."

From Sand Creek, Chivington sent a telegram to Major General Curtis at Fort Leavenworth to inform the general of his own small losses and claiming that his men had killed Black Kettle and other chiefs along with four or five hundred Indians. To justify his actions, he said that a fresh white scalp had been found in one of the natives' lodges, indicating they were hostiles. Chivington also sent a telegram to Governor Evans, who was currently in Washington, D.C., briefly detailing his exploits at Sand Creek. "Still after them," he reported. Chivington spent another day near Sand Creek, and then he and his men set out to try to find an Arapaho encampment on the Arkansas River. Fortunately, they had abandoned camp before Chivington's troops got there.

Nonetheless, an exultant Chivington was heard to say once back at Fort Lyon that they would put a star on his shoulder, meaning he would be promoted to brigadier general.

Chapter 4: Investigations of the Massacre

"[H]undreds of women and children were coming towards us and getting on their knees for mercy. Anthony shouted, 'Kill the sons of bitches' ... the massacre lasted six to eight hours...I refused to fire, and swore that none but a coward would, for by this time hundreds of women and children were coming towards us, and getting on their knees for mercy. I tell you Ned it was hard to see little children on their knees have their brains beat out by men professing to be civilized. Some tried to escape on the Prairie, but most of them were run down by horsemen ... They were all horribly mutilated. One women was cut open and child taken out of her, and scalped..." – Captain Silas S. Soule

Returning with his men to Denver on December 12th, Chivington was acclaimed as a great hero. Some of the 100 scalps brought back went on display as part of a theatrical performance, a sort of white version of the victorious scalp dance, and in a December 17 article, the *Rocky Mountain News* said only good things about the "Battle of Sand Creek:" The newspaper bragged, "Among the brilliant feats of arms in Indian warfare, the recent campaign of our Colorado volunteers will stand in history with few rivals and none to exceed in its final results." Chivington himself was lauded for his skill in moving his forces such a long distance in total secrecy and under such adverse winter weather conditions.

However, the notion that he and his men had covered themselves with glory in a great victory over hostile natives soon began to unravel. The real white hero of Sand Creek (if there were any) was Silas S. Soule, Captain of Company D 1st Regiment. Born in Maine, Soule came from a stout abolitionist background, and his family had moved to Kansas during the 1850s as part of a concerted effort by New Englanders to try to keep slavery out of that new territory. Soule may also have been involved in a plot to try to save a couple of John Brown's men after the raid on Harper's Ferry in 1859.

In 1860, as many young men did, he had ventured to Colorado to seek his fortune in the gold fields, and as a volunteer soldier when the Civil War broke out, he was serving as a lieutenant with the 1st Regiment at the aforementioned victorious actions against the Confederates in New Mexico. Stationed at Fort Lyon, he accompanied Major Wynkoop and the native chiefs to the pivotal meeting at Camp Weld in Denver. Subsequently, much to the anger and disgust of Chivington, he challenged his superior officers on taking part in an expedition to kill natives whom he considered to be under the military's protection. Convinced to go along to Sandy Creek by Major Anthony telling him that they were going to fight hostiles at Smoky Creek, he ordered his own men away from what he later described as an out-of-control mob. That said, it must be noted that Soule explained he had moved his men away because they were in a deadly crossfire between soldiers who were on both banks of the creek trying to kill natives beneath.

Soule

Two week after Sand Creek, Soule wrote a letter to his friend and former commanding officer at Fort Lyon, the sidelined Major Wynkoop, expressing deep distress about what he had seen there, and through the abolitionist networks, a very different story soon reached the East Coast. On January 13, 1865, Massachusetts Senator Charles Sumner rose up in the Senate to denounce what he heard had transpired at Sand Creek as an "exceptional crime" which the Senate should be swift in punishing. Throughout that year, three investigations of what happened at Sand Creek were conducted: one by the military and two by Congress. Before long, Chivington was being called a barbarous murderer in some newspapers back east.

The military's investigation convened in Denver on February 1, 1865 and, including a trip to Fort Lyon, continued steadily until the end of May. The members of the commission were three veteran officers from the 1st Colorado Cavalry, and the commission, whose hearings were held in private, was not a trial but an attempt to accumulate facts and "fix the responsibility, if any, and to insure justice to all parties." It was tasked with determining whether the natives were under the protection of the military, whether Chivington had known that fact, and whether he had taken any actions or to prevent "unnatural outrages" by his command and to punish any transgressors. The commission was also interested in the disposition of the property captured from the natives, much of which had after disappeared.

The work of the commission was hampered somewhat because many of the cavalrymen at Sand Creek were 100-day men and were no longer serving in the military. Moreover, Major Anthony resigned from the military at the end of January, and Chivington would resign in February.

From the outset, Chivington attempted a series of legal maneuvers, including: requesting that the hearings be delayed to give him more opportunity to prepare; that they be opened to the public with newspaper reporters allowed to be present; opposing the inclusion on the commission of Lieutenant Colonel S. F. Tappan, who he said was prejudicial to him and had already made known he thought what had happened at Sand Creek was disgraceful; and, finally, asserting the commission lacked the proper authority to investigate the matter, which should go to a court of inquiry instead.

After some consideration, those requests were denied, and the commission proceeded on February 15th to call its first witness, Captain Soule. Soule, a highly hostile witness against Chivington, was well-informed given that he was present at the parley between Major Wynkoop and the natives, present at the subsequent talks in Denver, and present at the Sand Creek massacre (where he moved his men away from the scene). Soule said that upon receiving a report of some horsemen approaching Fort Lyon, he had met Chivington and his expedition some distance away and had conversations with them. When he mentioned the presence at the fort of Indian "prisoners," one man had said in return that they would not soon be prisoners. When he learned that the objective of the expedition was an attack on the Indians camped at Sandy Creek, Soule protested to his own superior officer, Major Anthony, and wrote a letter of protest to Chivington that was delivered by another officer. He testified that Major Anthony said to him that he was for killing all of the natives and had only been acting friendly with them until a superior force had arrived.

At Sand Creek, Soule testified that he had seen natives with their hands up approach the troops to indicate they were friends. He also testified that he had seen women and children being shot, scalped, and mutilated and that the commanding officers had made no effort to stop it. When he had made a second visit to Sand Creek with an inspection tour of the scene on December 31, 1864, he saw the bodies of 69 natives still lying there, all of whom had been scalped and mutilated. Finally, he gave testimony about specific cavalrymen who had property in their possession. Under cross-examination by Chivington, Soule said after the battle that a number of his fellow officers back at Fort Lyon had expressed their view that Chivington ought to be prosecuted.

After six days, during which the commissioners questioned Soule and some cross-examination was done by Colonel Chivington, the next witness called was 2nd Lt. Joseph D. Cramer of Company D, 1st Cavalry Regiment. This was also a multi-day interview, and like Soule, Cramer said that he had protested the expedition to Sand Creek, feeling that it was dishonorable to violate the promises made to the natives. He had been the officer ordered by Chivington to burn the encampment, and a damaging piece of evidence against Chivington in his testimony was that Captain Cree had said in his presence at Sand Creek that Chivington had said to kill any prisoners.

James P. Beckwith testified next. He was brought along on the expedition as a guide and interpreter, and he testified that Colonel Chivington had waved the bloody shirt as they were going into battle: "I don't tell you to kill all ages and sex, but look back on the plains of the Platte, where your mothers, fathers, brothers, sisters have been slain, and their blood saturating the sands on the Platte." Beckwith also testified that all sexes and ages of Indians had been killed, from one week-old babies to 80-year olds, and that they had all been scalped. Two-thirds were women and children. He saw White Antelope (a chief) he knew well running towards Chivington with his hands up and yelling in English, "Stop! Stop!" For his troubles trying to prevent any violence, White Antelope was shot dead.

In early January following the massacre, Beckwith had visited a mixed Cheyenne and other Indian village near Smoky Hill. Asked by the commissioners what the Indians there had to say, Beckwith said, over the objections of Chivington (who argued that the statements of Native Americans had no legal standing), that he had tried to convince the natives he met in council to sue for peace because the whites were too numerous. What he heard back in response was, "We know it. But what do we want to live for? The white man has taken our country, killed all of our game; was not satisfied with that, but killed our wives and children. Now no peace. We want to go and meet our families in the spirit land. We loved the whites until we found out they lied to us, and robbed us of what we had. We have raised the battle-ax until death."

In his cross-examination, Chivington insinuated that since Beckwith was not of the white race -- he was an African-American who had been born into slavery in Virginia and had been adopted later by the Crow Indians -- his testimony was invalid. However, this was ruled out of order by the commissioners.

Private Naman D. Snyder of Company D, 1st Regiment – Capt. Soule's Company – testified he had seen the American flag being displayed by the natives over the village. He also asserted that he had witnessed plenty of scalping done by the "boys" in the 1st and 3rd Regiments and by some "Mexicans" (a small detachment of the 1st New Mexico Cavalry) whom he thought were with Chivington. In January, Snyder had been one of those who had gone back to Sand Creek with Soule and others on the trip to inspect the scene of the massacre. In his cross-examination, Chivington, now clutching at straws, tried unsuccessfully to get Snyder to admit that the condition of the bodies still lying there on the battlefield had been altered.

On March 20, the commission reconvened at Fort Lyon. At the fort, testimony was taken first with the key actor, Major Wynkoop, who was once again in command of the post. Wynkoop reviewed the events he had taken part in leading up to Sand Creek, starting with the letters he had received from Black Kettle and other chiefs asking for a parley to make peace and to enable an exchange of prisoners. He related how, from what he had learned of the natives' perspective, warfare had begun due to a series of missteps made by the whites. Regarding what happened at the conference held in Denver, Wynkoop attested that both Governor Evans and Colonel Chivington (who presented himself to the natives as the "big war chief of this part of the country" and in the "business" of killing Indians) left matters concerning them to Wynkoop's discretion until the higher command could be heard from. Thus, Wynkoop told the chiefs to bring in their villages with "their squaws and papooses…under assurances of perfect safety and protection from the government" to the vicinity of Fort Lyon, where he could keep an eye on them and make sure no "depredations" were committed. The natives "were perfectly satisfied with the assurances that I had given them," and since they were in a destitute condition, Wynkoop said he would occasionally issue them some rations.

When Wynkoop was relieved of his command and turned it over to Major Anthony on the 5th of November, Anthony told him he was under strict instructions to have nothing to do with the natives. However, after being informed of the situation by Wynkoop, he agreed to follow almost the same course as Wynkoop. One difference is that Anthony demanded that the natives turn in their weapons, which at least some of them did (although mainly older guns). Wynkoop said he was present when Major Anthony consulted with the chiefs of the Cheyenne and Arapaho and heard Anthony tell them he would accord them the very same protection until he got word from the commanding general of the department.

Overall, the testimony taken by the commission at Fort Lyon presents an exceedingly ugly picture of Colonel Chivington as a man who was obsessed with killing natives and using it to achieve fame and glory for himself. Before the massacre, Chivington, in the presence of officers at the fort, had denounced anybody who would advocate peace with the natives and declared he would soon be "wading in [their] gore" and that "scalps are what we are after." Following the massacre, Chivington was heard to have expressed pleasure that 500 or 600 Indians been killed, which made it the largest-ever "battle" with Native Americans to that point. In a report on the situation written to his superior officer after resuming command of Fort Lyon in January, Major Wynkoop referred to Chivington as an "inhuman monster" who had committed an "unprecedented atrocity" and talked about how difficult this had made relations with the local natives. Anyone who reads the hundreds of pages of testimony given in this and the other two investigations of Sand Creek, it is hard to disagree with that characterization.

Chivington tried repeatedly to undermine the testimony of the soldiers by suggesting that the mutilation of the Indian bodies was actually the work of dogs or wolves. One witness replied, "I don't hardly think that dogs or wolves could chaw the scalp off and leave the body alone." The same witness reported seeing several of the officers involved with men in the scalping. All witnesses were in agreement that they had heard no orders from Chivington to stop.

Returning to Denver from Fort Lyon on April 20th, the commission next heard from a series of witnesses whom Chivington hoped would be sympathetic ones, but this was not necessarily the case. Colonel George Shoup of the 3rd Colorado Cavalry, Chivington's immediate subordinate, after describing the role his regiment had played at Sand Creek, admitted under sharp questioning by the commissioners that he had in fact seen "one or two men" who were in the act of scalping and that he had heard Chivington say he did not intend to take any of the natives prisoner.

Chivington tried hard to discredit the main hostile witnesses. He asked for a deposition to be taken from a Jewish wagon train "freighter," Lipman Meyer, which described Soule as having been drunk and incompetent and having stolen his blankets when he encountered him and his cavalry detachment on the trail in December. B.N. Forbes of the 1st Cavalry Regiment, who had been present at the parley with the Indians in September, was brought in by Chivington to try to discredit Major Wynkoop. The accusations again involved excessive drink and military incompetence, plus a lack of confidence from those under his command. The commission, losing patience with these personal attacks on the witnesses, squelched an effort by Chivington to have yet another of his witnesses called to impeach another witness.

Another approach attempted by Chivington in the second round of hearings in Denver was trying to establish that he was himself a victim. He brought in Captain Theodore G. Cree, formerly of the 3rd Cavalry Regiment, to suggest there was among some officers a kind of conspiracy to get Chivington, a theory based on a conservation he reported having had with Lieutenant Cramer of the 1st Cavalry Regiment. Captain Presley Talbot of the 3rd Regiment testified that, while lying wounded, he overheard a conversation between Indian agent Colley and interpreter John Smith bemoaning the loss of thousands of dollars of buffalo robes and other goods destroyed in the battle and declaring they would "do anything to damn" Colonel Chivington or Major Downing. Smith was also heard by Talbot boasting that the Eastern newspapers would soon be full of letters from Fort Lyon about what had really happened at Sand Creek and that he would make every effort to have vengeance upon Chivington for having murdered his son.

To address the main allegation against Chivington that the natives attacked on Sand Creek were peaceful ones, trader S. P. Ashcraft testified at Chivington's behest that he knew Black Kettle's band of Cheyenne had been committing hostile acts and that the Sioux had told him all the Cheyenne were going to start a war. Chivington also tried to spread the responsibility among other commanding officers, using as a witness 2nd Lieutenant Harry Richmond, Company B of the 3rd Colorado Cavalry, who testified that he had "never heard [Major] Anthony express himself except exultingly over the battle of Sand creek or the arrival of troops to give battle."

Also testifying for Chivington, Private Alexander M. Safely of the 1st Cavalry said that he had been present shortly after their arrival at Ft. Lyon when Major Anthony thanked Chivington for coming and said he was eager to go out and fight the Indians at Sand Creek because he was becoming alarmed that they would come soon and attack the fort. However, the commissioners refused to let Chivington bring in Major Simeon Whitely, formerly of the 1st Cavalry, for a similar claim that Major Anthony had stated to Whitely that he thought the natives at Sand Creek were hostile and had urged Chivington to attack and kill them.

Chivington's most effective witnesses was probably Sergeant Stephen Decatur from the 3rd Regiment. Decatur testified that in his capacity as clerk, he had gone over the battlefield the following day and had counted 450 dead warriors. This pleased him and made him wish he had fought harder the day before, since, while the village was being burned the previous evening, he had witnessed soldiers opening bundles or bales from the natives that contained the scalps of white men, women and children, along with personal items like daguerreotypes, the wearing apparel of white women and children, and ladies' make-up. Decatur said he had a personal stake in making an accurate count because he had been at the Hungate farm and knew Mrs. Hungate and her children before they were slaughtered. Asked by the commission, Decatur claimed that he had not seen any scalping or mutilation and that he had not seen any white flag displayed by the Indians, as other witnesses stated. He said he saw a small number of women killed, mostly in the sand pits. He claimed, unlike other witnesses, that these pits must have been dug beforehand.

Dr. Caleb S. Birdsall, 1st Assistant Surgeon of the 3rd, testified that he examined some scalps that had been brought to him by a soldier and that, based on coloration, they were white scalps. One scalp appeared to be fresh, since it had moist skin and flesh attached to it. Dr. Thaddeus B. Bell, also present at Sand Creek, was called in by Chivington to further confirm the existence of the white scalps found on the battlefield, but no actual scalps were introduced into evidence. When asked about the location of the scalps, the witnesses were not able to be very helpful.

Colonel Chivington registered objections at almost every turn of the proceedings, but he did not testify in his own behalf. The military commission adjourned its work on May 30, 1865.

Meanwhile, 1500 miles from Denver in Washington, D.C., the Congress's Joint Committee on the Conduct of the War was holding its own hearings, starting on March 13. Chivington, under subpoena, gave written testimony for this one. First, he denied knowing that more than one woman was killed and claimed he had seen no dead children. He asserted the natives in the camp were hostiles by virtue of belonging to the same tribes that had committed "outrages" elsewhere on whites. He could not ascertain individual responsibility, especially given the "character" of Indians with respect to their truthfulness. The number of white scalps Chivington said were found in the camp at Sand Creek swelled from one (in his report made the day of the massacre) to 19 in his congressional testimony. He denied that the chiefs who came to Denver had been offered peace. Ultimately, the defense of his conduct rested on what in the mid-20th century would come to be known as the "Nuremberg Defense," the assertion that he could not go against the orders of his superior officer (Major General Curtis). In his congressional testimony's final words asking for vindication, Chivington presented himself and his men as having been dutiful defenders of "civilization."

However, most testimony given in Washington was hostile to Chivington. The first witness called to testify was the Indian agent, Jesse H. Leavenworth, a West Point graduate and son of the general for whom Fort Leavenworth, Kansas was named. He was not present at the massacre, but he asserted that he knew well the natives from Black Kettle's and White Antelope's bands who had gathered at Fort Lyon and that there never had been any more friendly to whites. He was followed by the Indian trader John S. Smith, who, as mentioned earlier, was present in Sand Creek on business when the massacre occurred. Among other atrocities committed by the soldiers, Smith described the murder of his own half-Cheyenne son, Jack, who was shot by a soldier the day after the massacre as he sat in his father's tent. Smith had gone to plead with Chivington for his life, and Chivington had refused to intervene.

Damaging testimony was also given by Captain S. M. Robbins, who was a member of Chivington's staff. He had been present at the "consultation" in Denver between the chiefs and Governor Evans and Chivington. His recollection was of the Governor telling the chiefs to show that their people were friendly by seeking the protection of the military posts, and that it was his understanding that at least some of the natives went to Fort Lyon to do just that. However, in partial justification for Chivington's actions, he described the feelings in Colorado at that time as being highly against natives and as wanting them all to be killed.

Colorado Governor and Indian Commissioner Evans, unlike with the Military Commission, appeared and gave testimony before the Joint Congressional Committee. Mainly, Evans pled ignorance due to his absence from the scene in Colorado following the September meeting with the chiefs in Denver, when he had turned the matter over to the military. When asked whether he thought there were any circumstances that justified Chivington's actions at Sand Creek, most likely thinking about how his words would play politically back home, Evans was evasive. The committee in its final report criticized him for his "prevarication."

Major Anthony also testified. He had seen one Indian being scalped, but he did not see any white scalps taken from them and had not heard anything about it in the 10 days he was with Chivington until Denver. He also testified about the young child being shot at by one soldier after another until he was killed. Asked if he approved of the attack on the natives at Sand Creek, he responded "no" because he thought it was a bad policy decision, not because it was immoral.

The Joint Congressional Committee concluded its work with language sharply critical of the anti-Indian sentiments in Colorado, which they felt was mostly responsible for the Sand Creek Massacre: "The hatred of the whites to the Indians would seem to have inflamed and excited to the utmost. The bodies of persons killed at a distance – whether by Indians or not is not certain – were brought to the capital of the Territory and exposed to the public gaze, for the purpose of inflaming still more the already excited feeling of the people."

Even as that Congressional investigation was ongoing, a third investigation was being conducted in Washington by a Joint Special Committee of the two houses of Congress as part of its overall work inquiring into the condition and treatment of the natives throughout the West. On March 7th, that committee began taking oral and written testimony on what it called "The Chivington Massacre." Some of the same persons testified as at the military's and the other Congressional investigation -- the Indian agent Samuel Colley, the interpreter John S. Smith, and Major Wynkoop from Fort Lyon – but many were different. All told, the committee received testimony from a total of 30 people.

One new witness of some interest who had not been heard from in the other investigations was Edmond G. Guierrer, the 25-year-old son of a French father and a Cheyenne mother who worked the Plains as a teamster and Indian trader. Guierrer had been with the natives at Sand Creek just four days prior to the attack, and he had spent a further four weeks with them in the period after the attack. He had come back to Sand Creek with John Smith to conduct trade and was present when the attack occurred, but he managed to escape by joining a native woman (his cousin) who was herding ponies away from the fighting. He was present at Smoky Creek later when the council held by the natives took count of those among them who had been killed and were missing. Thus, his figures may be the most accurate for the massacre's toll: 148 killed and missing, 60 of them men, the rest being women and children.

Witnesses were generally reluctant to name names, but Lieutenant James Olney of the 1st Colorado Cavalry testified he had seen eight prisoners, consisting of three "squaws" and five children, being led along when they were approached by Lieutenant Harry Richmond of the 3rd Colorado Cavalry. Richmond immediately shot and scalped them while they were crying out for mercy. The next day, Lt. Richmond was seen by another witness scalping two Indians. Perhaps not coincidentally, Richmond was one of the few officers who had testified on Chivington's behalf in Denver.

In a sworn written statement taken at Fort Lyon, Lieutenant Joseph D. Cramer testified to this second congressional investigating committee. He asserted that the claims about the natives at Sand Creek having had white scalps in their possession was a "mistake." He said he had only seen one scalp, "but it was very old, the hair being much faded." As the man who was ordered to burn the village, he had gone through all the lodges, so he was in a good position to know the real truth. Cramer also testified that he had been present at an "interview" between Major Anthony and the chiefs that had taken place three days before the massacre. The chiefs had come to the fort because they had heard from the Sioux that the 3rd Cavalry Regiment was advancing in their direction – which means Chivington's secrecy had failed – and they wanted their people to come in to the fort for protection. Anthony told them to stay put at Sand Creek. This piece of evidence suggests that he may have been setting up the natives.

In his testimony to this committee (sent by writing from Fort Lyon), Mayor Wynkoop blamed the causes of the difficulties on the incident involving Lieutenant Dunn and the allegedly stolen cattle. Before that, the natives had been totally peaceful. In fact, he said he was so confident that they were peaceful that he had visited them unescorted with his family.

Wynkoop also added another important bit of information for an understanding of the massacre's background that was not available otherwise. He had met privately with Governor Evans in Denver prior to the council meeting with the chiefs, and Wynkoop told the congressional committee that Evans was extremely reluctant to even meet with the chiefs. Evans had expressed concern to Wynkoop that if he were to make peace with the natives, it would not play well in Washington since he had just asked them to support the formation of one more regiment (the 100-day men in the 3rd) to go out and fight against them. Wynkoop reported that the "querulous" Evans asked, "What will I do with the 3rd Regiment?"

In an effort to refute the prevarication accusation made against him by the Joint Committee on the Conduct of the War, Evans submitted a "public letter" with supporting documents in a section by section rebuttal of that committee's report. Although he again stressed that he had had nothing to do with the "battle," the main thrust of his argument was that the chiefs with whom he had met in Denver had been responsible for committing hostile acts and were not peaceful ones as had been concluded by the Joint Congressional Committee. Evans protested, contrary to the other committee's report, that he had tried hard in his capacity as Indian superintendent to maintain peace with the natives but that his overtures were rejected.

One of the few witnesses giving outright testimony during this Congressional investigation in the defense of Colonel Chivington was Major Jacob Downing of the 1st Cavalry. Downing, a lawyer in civilian life, had acted as Chivington's attorney in the previous investigation. In the fighting at Sand Creek, he professed to have seen no flag displayed by the Indians and to have seen little or no scalping going on. At the same time, he made his views on Native Americans utterly clear: "I heard Colonel Chivington give no orders in regard to prisoners. I tried to take none myself, but killed all I could; and I think that was the general feeling in the command. I think and earnestly believe the Indians to be an obstacle to civilization, and should be exterminated."

The *Rocky Mountain News* railed against news of a congressional committee investigating Chivington and Sand Creek. It editorialized sarcastically, "By all means, let there be an investigation, but we advise the honorable congressional committee, who may be appointed to conduct it, to get their scalps insured before they pass Plum Creek on their way out." Plum Creek, Nebraska was where 40 white men in a freight wagon train had been attacked and killed on August 8, 1864, by a joint party of Sioux, Cheyenne and Arapaho warriors.

Meanwhile, the *New York Tribune* struck a different tone on March 31, 1865, saying of Sand Creek that it was "one of the most brutal and fiendish attacks" on Native Americans ever recorded. On August 8, 1865, Washington's *Evening Star* ran the headline "Negotiations with the Indians; The Sand Creek Butchery," with an article reporting that three U.S. Senators had just returned from the West after telling the natives that the government disapproved of Chivington's actions.

Not surprisingly, no Cheyennes or Arapahos were called to bear witness at any of the three investigations.

Chapter 5: Historical Consequence of the Massacre

The most important result for the natives and the United States is that the massacre damaged possibilities for peace. As trader and interpreter John S. Smith said in his testimony before Congress, the natives only wanted to kill whites after the massacre, and even he was afraid to go unaccompanied among them. Black Kettle lost all credibility with the other Cheyennes, who ridiculed him about why he had not remained at Sandy Creek to die with his brother, Little Antelope. Colonel James Ford wrote on May 31, 1865 from Fort Larned that all tribes of natives he knew were now hostile, and to counter the 7,000 mounted warriors he had heard were now operating south of the fort, he estimated he would need 10,000 men, with at least 4,000 of them mounted and constantly in the field. As he put it, "I have no doubt the attack of Colonel Chivington on the Cheyennes had a very bad effect."

During the spring and summer of 1865, war and peace factions struggled among both native groups and whites. There was a renewed push for strong punitive action from segments of the U.S. military, but they were overruled by the civilian establishment in Washington, which wanted a peace on the Western frontier to match the peace achieved at the end of the Civil War. Meanwhile, Black Kettle, in spite of everything the Cheyenne and the Arapaho had suffered, continued to push for peace. Thought by the whites to have been among those killed at Sand Creek, Black Kettle made an appearance at a peace conference in August attended by all of the main Plains tribes, and at the follow-up conference in October 1865, Major General John B. Sanborn, a member of the Indian Peace Commission appointed by Congress, announced that the Great White Father in Washington (President Andrew Johnson) wanted to offer reparations to the natives for what had happened at Sand Creek. Ironically, they were offered individual allotments of half and quarter sections as if they were settlers on their own land, but not where they had been living recently. Instead, they were offered lands south of the Arkansas River or north of the Platte River.

The Dog Soldiers were adamantly opposed to any new concessions, especially since it meant giving up their favorite hunting grounds for buffalo in the Smoky Hill River region. They and other Cheyenne were further angered when a military expedition in April 1867 burned a Cheyenne village near Fort Larned, Kansas, from which the inhabitants had fled due to memories of what had happened at Sand Creek. The next round of negotiations with the Indian Peace Commission was even less palatable among the militant Cheyenne because it involved having to move to a reserve in Oklahoma. Black Kettle and some other Indians did accept that offer, albeit with some reluctance, but the Dog Soldiers continued to make raids on settlements until they were defeated at the Battle of Summit Springs in Colorado in July 1869.

Colonel Chivington remained totally unrepentant about what had occurred at Sand Creek until the end of his life in 1894, and he continued to have many white defenders, particularly in Colorado. Chivington suffered no punishment for his crimes committed at Sand Creek, but his military and political aspirations were over, and he started an itinerant life, trying his hand at a number of different ventures (mostly unsuccessfully). He acquired some further notoriety for seducing and marrying his dead son's widow, who a few years later divorced him for non-support. His application for a government pension was refused, and at the time of his death, some newspapers around the country took note of both his achievements in fighting the Confederates in New Mexico and his butchery of the natives at Sand Creek, atrocities that the *New Orleans Times-Picayune* opined "were never equaled by the Indians themselves."

By then, the term "massacre" was being commonly invoked for Sand Creek, while the Congressional committees had used it immediately, but with Chivington's death coming four years after the 1890 census had declared the end of the western frontier, newspapers were much more interested in what was happening with the economic depression and Coxey's Army as they made their way to Washington to demand relief. Chivington's name lives on today as the name of a small town in Kiowa County, Colorado that is located just 15 miles from the site of the massacre.

Due to Sand Creek, John Evans was asked by President Andrew Johnson in July 1865 to resign his job as territorial governor, but he remained popular in Colorado until his death in Denver in 1897. In recent years, both the University of Denver and Northwestern University have opened investigations into the massacre's history and have sought to come to terms with his involvement.

Captain Silas Soule, who had taken the job of provost marshal, was assassinated on the streets of Denver within two months of giving testimony against Chivington. He was just 26. The killer or killers were never identified, although it is presumed that they were upset at Soule for testifying, and Soule had confided to a friend that he feared personal harm would come to him as a result. In 2010, the Colorado Historical Society unveiled a commemorative plaque on the street corner (15th and Arapaho) where he was shot dead. In part, it commended him for ordering his men not to shoot at the natives and for later testifying against his commander and detailing the atrocities committed by the troops at Sand Creek. In December 2014, Cheyenne and Arapaho held a ceremony at Soule's Denver grave site and also honored Lieutenant Joseph Cramer.

Chivington's other principal critic, Major Edward Wynkoop, became a government Indian agent in 1866, and the Southern Cheyenne and Arapaho thereby became his official charges. In December 1868, he took another righteous moral stand by resigning this position as Indian agent to protest the destruction of another Cheyenne village, the village where Black Kettle was living on the Washita River in western Oklahoma. That action on Wynkoop's part brought an end to his praiseworthy public career as someone who tried hard to do the right thing. Wynkoop's life is the subject of a biography by Louis Kraft, *Ned Wynkoop and the Lonely Road from Sand Creek* (2011).

As perhaps the most famous chief at Sand Creek, it's somewhat ironic that Black Kettle was killed in the attack of the camp on the Washita River years after the Sand Creek Massacre. That attack was led by George Armstrong Custer, a Civil War cavalry veteran who would earn greater infamy among Native Americans than Chivington. Of course, Custer is best remembered for dying at the hands of Sioux and Cheyenne warriors at Little Big Horn in 1876.

Sand Creek and its meaning for American history again became a matter of public discussion and some contention during the 1990s when a campaign by the Cheyenne and the Arapaho was successful in 2000 in having a National Historic Site established at Sand Creek. The efforts were led in Congress by U.S. Senator from Colorado, Ben Nighthorse Campbell, a Cheyenne. Some conservatives preferred calling it a "battlefield" like Yorktown or Gettysburg, but the use of the name "Sand Creek Massacre National Historic Site" prevailed. It is the only site in the vast National Park System that memorialized a massacre of Native Americans.

Campbell

A memorial plaque at the site of the massacre

A lot has been written about the Sand Creek Massacre. Two books that cover the political controversies around the establishment of the National Historic Site are Ari Kelman's *A Misplaced Massacre: Struggling Over the Memory of Sand Creek* (2013), and *Finding Sand Creek: History, Archeology, and the 1864 Massacre Site* (2013), authored by Jerome A. Greene and Douglas D. Scott. Other full-length book treatments include *Month of the Freezing Moon: The Sand Creek Massacre, November 1864* (1991) by Duane P. Schultz; *Blood at Sand Creek: The Massacre Revisited* (1994) by Bob Scott; *The Massacre at Sand Creek: Narrative Voices* (1995) by Bruce Cutler; *Battle at Sand Creek: The Military Perspective* (2004) by Gregory F. Michno; and *Forgotten Heroes and Villains of Sand Creek* (2010) by Carol Turner.

While the U.S. government has never officially apologized for Sand Creek as it has done for the internment of Japanese-Americans during World War II and for not informing or treating Southern black sharecroppers infected with syphilis as part of a U.S. Public Health Service study, the military and congressional investigations of Sand Creek that took place in 1865 might be seen as early examples of what have come to be called "Truth Commissions." These kinds of commissions have been established in recent years by countries like South Africa and Guatemala to bring facts to light and come to terms with egregious human rights violations. The main difference, of course, is that the human rights victims at Sand Creek were not present to provide testimony of their suffering or confront their perpetrators in a courtroom.

According to the 2010 census, less than 2% of Colorado's population is Native American, and no Cheyenne or Arapaho reservations exist in the state. Indeed, there are only two reservations, both held by the Utes. The Northern Cheyenne have a reservation in southeastern Montana, and many Southern Cheyenne live in the area of their former reservation in Oklahoma. For their part, the Northern Arapaho share the Wind River Reservation in Wyoming with the Eastern Shoshone. Many Americans still have little or no knowledge about Sand Creek, but many Native Americans still consider it one of their most painful historical memories, right alongside Wounded Knee in 1890.

Bibliography

Annual Report of the Commissioner of Indian Affairs for the Year 1864. Washington D.C.: Government Printing Office, 1865.

Grinnell, George Bird. *The Cheyenne Indians: Their History and Ways of Life*. Vol. 1. Lincoln: University of Nebraska Press, 1972.

———. *The Fighting Cheyennes*. New York: C. Scribner's Sons, 1915.

Hall, Frank. *History of the State of Colorado*. Vol. 4. Chicago: Blakely Printing Company, 1889.

Hatch, Thom. *Black Kettle : The Cheyenne Chief Who Sought Peace but Found War*. Hoboken, N.J: Wiley, 2004.

Kappler, Charles J., ed. *Indian Affairs: Laws and Treaties*. Washington D.C.: Government Printing Office, 1903.

"Massacre of the Cheyenne Indians." In *Report of the Joint Committee on the Conduct of the War, at the Second Session Thirty-Eighth Congress*. Washington, D.C: Government Printing Office, 1865.

Mooney, James. *The Cheyenne Indians*. Published for the American Anthropological Association, 1905.

"Sand Creek Massacre." In *Senate Documents, Otherwise Publ. as Public Documents and Executive Documents: 14th Congress, 1st Session-48th Congress, 2nd Session and Special Session*. Washington D.C.: Government Printing Office, 1867.

Sturtevant, William C. *Handbook of North American Indians: Plains*. Vol. 2. Washington D.C.: Smithsonian Institution, 2001.

"The Chivington Massacre." In *Condition of the Indian Tribes: Report of the Joint Special Committee, Appointed Under Joint Resolution of March 3, 1865: With an Appendix*. Washington

D.C.: Government Printing Office, 1867.

Utley, Robert Marshall. *The Indian Frontier of the American West, 1846-1890.* 1st ed. *Histories of the American Frontier.* Albuquerque: University of New Mexico Press, 1984.

The Wounded Knee Massacre

Chapter 1: The Great Sioux War of 1876-1877

In 1868, the U.S. government entered into a treaty with Lakota Sioux and Arapaho leaders at Fort Laramie, which allegedly guaranteed that the Lakota people would own the Black Hills (Paha Sapa) of South Dakota in perpetuity, and that area would be set aside for Native Americans only. Whites could not enter the territory without the express permission of the Sioux. This was essential, because the Black Hills are the "holy land" of Lakota and other indigenous peoples. In addition, the Treaty of Fort Laramie dictated that the U.S. Army would abandon forts along the Bozeman Trail.

However, because none of the chiefs could read English, the content of the treaty was merely "explained" to them, and most of the explanation consisted of lies and half truths. In reality, the treaty provided for reservations – where the Native Americans would live – and the cession of certain tribal lands to the United States. In 1870, Sioux chief Red Cloud traveled to New York City and Washington D.C., speaking to crowds and explaining both his people's plight and his understanding of the Treaty of Fort Laramie of 1868. It was during this trip that he became convinced that his people could never overcome the American settlers, based on their numbers and their great cities. However, his speeches in the east were sufficient to raise public awareness and led to the alteration of the original treaty. An Indian Agency was also established on the North Platte River in 1873, expressly for the Oglala Sioux. Because the Red Cloud Agency was established, the distribution of food and goods promised to Sioux bands by the Treaty of Fort Laramie of 1868 could be delivered and distributed to the Native Americans. The following year, the U.S. Army established Camp Robinson near the Red Cloud Agency to both protect the agency and keep a watchful eye on the Oglala.

Meanwhile, the treaty itself was broken almost immediately. When an expedition into the Black Hills led by Lieutenant Colonel George Custer discovered gold in 1874, miners flooded into the region in violation of the treaty. Lakota people, hunting within the confines of the territory promised to them by the Fort Laramie Treaty of 1868, began encountering white settlers and attacked them. In response, whites demanded protection by the U.S. Army, which had been complying with the treaty and ejected the white interlopers.

Custer

The removal of white miners had the effect of increasing political pressure on the government to open the Black Hills to mining, logging, and settlement. In May 1875, several Lakota leaders traveled to Washington D.C. in the hope of convincing President Ulysses S. Grant to honor the treaty conditions. They were unsuccessful, and the government attempted to purchase the Black Hills for $25,000.00. Late in the fall of the same year, Grant met with Major General Philip Sheridan and Brigadier General George Crook and the three agreed to end the policy of ejecting miners and settlers. Also, the President and the generals decided to notify Native American bands not already residing on the reservation that they had until January 31, 1876, to surrender to authorities and settle on reservations. Among these "non-treaty" bands were those led by Crazy Horse and Sitting Bull. The concept of ultimatums was foreign to Native Americans, and many bands were so far from existing reservations that they would be hard pressed to make it onto reservations before the deadline had passed even if they wanted to.

During the first half of 1876, the U.S. Army sent soldiers into the region to deal with the Native Americans who had not surrendered or moved to the reservation, leading to the fateful Battle of the Little Bighorn. On the morning of June 25, 1876, George Custer's scouts discovered a Native American village about 15 miles away in the valley of the Little Bighorn River. Choosing to disregard his superiors' orders to wait for a concerted effort, the grandstanding Custer intended to deliver his own decisive victory by dividing his command into three units, an extremely bold tactic when done in the face of a much larger force. Due to their belief in the inferiority of the Plains Indians, and mindful of previous Indian tactics that sought to avoid pitched battle, Custer and his men were most concerned with forcing the action and failed to understand the true nature of the situation they had entered. The Native American gathering, centered around the famous Sioux chief Sitting Bull, numbered roughly 8,000 individuals, and about 2,000 of them were warriors. Custer's forces amounted to a mere 31 officers, 566 troopers, and 50 scouts and civilians, and they had been split into three columns in order to stop a possible retreat.

Before the battle, it is believed Custer thought he was facing a group of about 800, which was Sitting Bull's strength in the weeks before the battle. However, the Army's Native American scouts and civilian scouts had not adequately informed the Army of the reinforcements that arrived, and at Little Bighorn, Custer's three-pronged attack was completely overwhelmed. How Custer met his fate, and whether there even was a Last Stand, remain subjects of debate, but what is known is that the Battle of the Little Bighorn was one of the U.S. military's biggest debacles. All told, the 7th Cavalry suffered over 50% casualties, with over 250 men killed and over 50 wounded. The dead included Custer's brothers Boston and Thomas, his brother-in-law James Calhoun, and his nephew Henry Reed. Custer and his men were buried where they fell. A year later, Custer's remains (or more accurately, the remains found in the spot labeled with his name) were relocated to West Point for final interment.

After the Battle of the Little Bighorn, the massive Teton, Lakota, and Cheyenne warrior-army disbanded, and in many ways, the battle, despite being a huge victory for the Native Americans, represented a portent of the coming destruction of the Native American warrior societies and their associated cultures.

In the aftermath of the 7th Cavalry's decimation and the complete destruction of Custer's force, the American public was incensed. The people's ire was probably inflamed by the fact that news reached the eastern United States just as the nation was celebrating its centennial. The nation's reaction was inflammatory and largely reflected the attitudes of the commanders in the field. U.S. troopers had assumed their own inherent eugenic and military superiority over Native Americans and had fully bought into the idea of "manifest destiny." In the months following this battle, the single greatest Native American victory against U.S. troops, the U.S. military sent thousands of cavalry troopers into the region seeking revenge for the "Custer Massacre." Native Americans involved in the battle referred to it as the Battle of the Greasy Grass, referring to the area where the fight happened.

Perhaps realizing that the Army would launch reprisals against them, the huge Native American camp disbanded and scattered. The response the Native Americans feared came quickly, and soon U.S. troops were flooding into Lakota territory. Sitting Bull, ever the tactical leader, knew the end was near and, refusing to surrender, led his people north. Eventually (by May of 1877), he led his people across the border and into Canada, which he called the home of the "Great Mother," referring to Queen Victoria. General Terry, the Chief's one-time military rival, ventured north and offered Sitting Bull surrender terms, but the Chief angrily sent him away.

Meanwhile, others, including Crazy Horse, continued to remain defiant. In early September, Captain Anson Mills and about 150 troopers from the 3rd Cavalry Regiment located a village of about three dozen Cheyenne lodges led by American Horse and attacked it the following morning. The Lakota who escaped the battle fled and warned nearby villages, including one where Crazy Horse and 600 to 800 warriors were living. The fleeing Native Americans said they had been attacked by 100 to 150 troops.

Crazy Horse's camp, located on the Tongue River (near present-day Birney, Montana), was populated by about 3,500 Lakota and Cheyenne peoples and included survivors of the Dull Knife Fight. Approaching Crazy Horse's camp was General Nelson Miles, who had driven Sitting Bull and his band into Canada in December of 1876. Seeing the condition of the Cheyenne survivors and considering the approach of winter, Crazy Horse had decided to attempt to negotiate the surrender of his band. However, the delegation he sent to inform Army officers of his pending surrender was attacked and killed by overzealous Army Crow scouts. This action greatly angered Crazy Horse, and he decided that revenge was necessary.

Nelson Miles

Thus, the war chief began a series of raids against Army outposts in an effort to draw General Miles away from his post. Miles led a mixed force of cavalry, infantry, and artillery into the Wolf Mountain area and set up a defensive perimeter on a ridgeline in three feet of snow. Early on the morning of January 8, 1877, Crazy Horse and Two Moons led a force of about 500 warriors in attacks on the soldiers' perimeter. Skillfully using his artillery and superior firepower, Miles was able to frustrate the repeated Native American attacks. Additionally, Miles was able to shift his reserves to cover his flanks when the warriors attempted to outflank his line. The General then ordered an advance and seized a ridge that allowed him to attack Native American positions with his artillery. Throughout the battle, the weather gradually grew worse, and soon Crazy Horse and his warriors withdrew.

Though the battle was indecisive, it was the last major engagement of the Great Sioux War of 1876-77. Also, the battle showed that Native American settlements were vulnerable to the U.S. Army even in the harsh conditions of the Plains winter. Over the next few months, Native Americans who had been following Crazy Horse began slipping away and returning to their reservations. Throughout the winter, Crazy Horse's people struggled, and by May of 1877, the weary leader led his people to the Red Cloud Agency near Fort Robinson, Nebraska, to surrender.

Chapter 2: The Ghost Dance

The Great Sioux War had ended over a decade earlier, but in the fall of 1889, word spread throughout Native American groups about a messiah who promised to lead all Indians into a new world without white men. By the time the stories about this new messiah reached the Lakota Sioux, they had been passed from tribe to tribe, most notably through the Arapahos and Shoshone of Wyoming. Because they had passed through so many tribes, the stories varied quite a bit, but the basic message remained the same: the messiah told of the return of the buffalo and other animals that had disappeared from tribal lands, and that Indian ancestors would also return to the world.

Understandably, the story appealed greatly to Native Americans whose world had been turned upside down during American migration to the West, and the idea of a return to traditional life was especially enticing because of the problems they had experienced on the reservations they had been confined to. In order to discuss the stories that were making their way through the Lakota people, the leaders of the Oglala Sioux organized a meeting at Pine Ridge, a meeting that involved many important tribal leaders, such as Kicking Bear, Red Cloud, Little Wound, American Horse and Young-Man-Afraid-of-His-Horses. During this meeting, the Oglalas created an eight person delegation that would travel west to find the messiah. The men chosen for the delegation included Good Thunder, who would head the group, as well as Yellow Knife, Flat Iron, Kicks Back, Elk Horn, Yellow Breast, Broken Arm, and Cloud Horse. Meanwhile, other Lakota groups appointed their own members to join the delegation. From the Rosebud Brulès, Short Bull and Mash-the-Kettle were appointed, while Kicking Bear would represent the Minneconjou.

Kicking Bear

The delegation left the Dakota Territory in secret, because they did not want to tip off U.S. Indian agents and also because they were technically not allowed to leave their reservations without approval from the government. Eventually, the delegation made its way along the southern boundary of the Black Hills and then moved into Wyoming Territory, following the North Platte River and making their way into the Indian villages around Fort Washakie. While staying there, they came across more delegations that were also traveling to see the messiah. It was decided that three Cheyenne and several Wind River Indians would join the Lakota delegation as they made their way westward.

The now-larger delegation first went by rail to Fort Hall in Idaho Territory, and at For Hall, they discovered an extremely high level of excitement there due to delegations of Bannock and

Shoshoni who had just returned from a trip to the Sierra Nevadas to hear the message of this new Indian Redeemer. It was here that the Lakota were told that the messiah advocated something called the *Dance of the Ghosts*, and that it would eventually bring the spirits of dead ancestors back to earth, where they would be alive once again. For American administrators at the forts surrounding the Sierra Nevadas, the Ghost Dance movement was not particularly concerning because there were no hints that the messiah's message advocated rebellion; in fact, according to the movement, he preached a message of peace. This also was not the first Indian revival but one of a series of revivals that had captured the attention of Native Americans across the continent and on reservations.

An 1890 sketch of Oglala Sioux performing the Ghost Dance

From Fort Hall, the delegation boarded another train, reaching Salt Lake City before traveling across Utah and into Nevada, where they eventually arrived at Pyramid Lake. Pyramid Lake was the gathering spot of a large crowd of Paiutes, Crows, and Southern Cheyennes who were waiting for the messiah. The delegation was welcomed by the crowd, where they began to learn about the messiah and his message in more detail. The messiah, whose actual name was Wovoka, told a story that was made up of a mixture of myths from various religious beliefs, but with two important strands coming out of Indian lore and also Christianity.

Wovoka

The origins of the movement came after Wovoka had a revelation while delirious during a bad fever. He had been taken to "the other world", where he saw God and also many tribal ancestors, who were all young and happy. According to Wovoka, God told him to tell his people to love one another and to live peacefully, both among themselves and with the white men. God then "gave" Wovoka a dance, and he was instructed to teach it to his people. They were to perform the dance periodically for the next few years, until the "renewal of the earth" occurred. The dance would take up five days: on the first day, the natives would fast and purify themselves in preparation. Then, from the second to the fifth day, they would dance.

Wovoka did not believe he was the son of God but rather a prophet passing along a divine revelation. However, his story grew as it was passed from person to person, and eventually he decided it was too difficult to correct the mistakes, especially in terms of the stories of his relationship to God as well as the miracles he had performed. Finally, the crowd around Pyramid Lake remained for a number of days until they were told that Wovoka, the messiah himself, would make an appearance at Walker Lake 100 miles to the south. At Walker Lake, the crowd that gathered was composed mainly of Native Americans but also included a number of whites who were curious as to what was occurring. When the messiah entered the area, he was surrounded by a group of Indians who were all wearing white men's clothing, and according to Porcupine, one of the Cheyenne companions of the Lakota, "I thought the Great Father was a white man...but this man looks like an Indian!"

Wovoka then spoke to the crowd:

> "My children, I am very glad to see you all. I sent for you and you have come. I am going to talk to you after a while about your relatives who are dead and gone...My children, I want you to listen to everything I have to say. I will teach you, also, how to dance a dance, and I want you to dance it faithfully from now on.
>
> In another spring or two the Great Spirit is coming. He is going to bring back game of every kind, so that it will be thick everywhere. All dead Indians will be strong and young again. Old, blind Indians will be able to see again.
>
> When the Great Spirit comes this way, all Indians will go away up high into a land where no one can hurt them any more. A big flood will come and all the evil people will be drowned. They will die. Later the water will go away and there will be no one but good people anywhere. All kinds of game will be plentiful.
>
> Now I want you to get the word to all Indians everywhere to keep dancing until this time of judgment comes." (Seymour, p.32)

Wovoka led the dance for a time before becoming tired, but the dance continued for hours without him, and the crowd danced until they were overcome by exhaustion. They laid down to rest, and upon waking, many of them reported seeing visions that confirmed the message of Wovoka. Wovoka's parting words emphasized the idea of peace:

> "My children...when you get home, go to farming and send your children to school. Do nothing wrong, and especially do not steal. People cannot take anything away with them when they die. And whisky is bad; those who drink it cause murders and suicides. Someday our Father, God, will look down and those who have done wrong will be shaken from the earth...My Father has given you back your old life...When you get home I want you to tell your people to follow my example. Any Indian who does not obey me will be buried under a new land which will grow over this old one when the earth is renewed. You people, all of you, use the paints and sagebrush I have given you. In the spring when the grass is green, your people who have gone before will all return, and you will see all your old friends because you came at my bidding. Even the buffalo, if you should kill one, will come to life again if you leave the head, the tail, and the feet." (Seymour, p.32-33)

The Lakota delegation returned to Pine Ridge in March 1890, and the messianic message that they brought back was enticing to the Lakota because of its promise to bring back the traditional way of life during a period of intense change. Two important Lakota who passed along Wovoka's message were Short Bull and Mash-the-Kettle, but in their telling, they minimized the pacifism of the message and instead focused on the destruction of all white men as well as the importance of continuously performing the ghost dance so that God could tell the faithful from the unfaithful.

Meanwhile, Kicking Bear also played an important role in bringing the ghost dance to the Lakota. Kicking Bear was able to play on the anger of some Lakota over the lack of supplies that the government had promised them to form a camp on Porcupine Creek that contained about 150 dancers. He also helped set up another camp nearby, led by Torn Belly and Jack Red Cloud, which contained 600 dancers. Kicking Bear recounted his journey to see the messiah, which was infused with mythic imagery and symbolism that appealed to his listeners:

> "In my tepee on the Cheyenne reservation, I arose many moons ago and prepared for a long journey. I had been told by a voice to go forth and meet the ghosts, because they were preparing to return and inhabit the earth. I traveled on the iron cars of the white man until I came to the place where the railroad ends. There I met two Indians whom I had never seen before, but who greeted me as a brother and gave me meat and bread. They had horses, and we rode without talking for four days, for I knew they would be witnesses to what I would see.
>
> Two suns we had traveled and had passed the last sign of white men -- for no white man had the courage to travel so far! -- when we saw a strange and fierce-looking black man, dressed in skins. He lived alone, and had medicine with which he could do anything he wished. He would wave his hands and make great heaps of money. Or, he would make another motion, and there before us would be many spring wagons, all painted and ready to hitch horses to. And still another motion of his hands and there sprung up before us great herds of buffalo!
>
> The black man spoke to us and told us that he was a friend of the Indian, that we should remain with him and go no farther, and that we could have all we wanted of the money, spring wagons, and buffalo.
>
> But we saw that we were being tempted from our purpose, and so our hearts were turned away from the black man, my brothers. We left him, and traveled for two more days.
>
> On the evening of the fourth day, when we were weak and faint from our journey, we looked for a camping place and were met by a man who was dressed like an Indian, but whose hair was long and glistening like the yellow money of the white man. His face was beautiful, and when he spoke my heard was glad and I forgot my hunger and the toil I had gone through. He said, 'Hau, my children, you have done well to make this long journey to come here. Leave your horses and follow me.

And our hearts sang in our breasts. And he led us up a great ladder of small clouds until we followed him through an opening in the sky --

My brothers, the tongue of Kicking Bear is straight, but he cannot tell all that he saw, because he is not an orator, but only the forerunner and herald of the ghosts. The one whom we followed took us to the Great Spirit and his wife, and we lay prostrate on the ground, but I saw that they were dressed as Indians!

Then from an opening in the sky we were shown all the countries of the earth, and the camping-grounds of our fathers since the beginning. All were there -- the tepees, the ghosts of our fathers, the great herds of buffalo, and a country that smiled because it was lush and rich...And the white man was not there!

Then he who showed us his hands and feet, and there were wounds in them which had been made by the white men when he went to them and they crucified him. And he told us he was going to come on earth again, only this time he would remain and live with the Indians, because they were his chosen people!

Then we were seated on rich skins, from animals which were unknown to me, in front of the open door of the Great Spirit's tepee. And we were told how to say the prayers and perform the dance that I have no come to show my brothers. And the Great Spirit spoke to us, saying:

'Take this message to my red children and tell it to them as I say it. I have neglected the Indians for many moons, but now I will make them my people if they obey me in this message. The earth is getting old and I will make it new for my chosen people, the Indians, who are going to inhabit it. And among them will be all of their ancestors who have died, their fathers, mothers, brothers, cousins and wives -- all those who hear my voice through the tongues of my children...

And while my children are dancing and preparing to join the ghosts, they shall have no fear of the white man, for I will take from him the secret of making gunpowder! And nay gunpowder they have on hand will not burn when it is directed against my children, the red people, who have learned the song and dance of the ghosts. But the powder which my children have will burn and kill when it is directed against the white man by those who believe! And if a red man should die at the hands of a white man while he is dancing, his spirit will only go to the end of the earth, join the ghosts of his fathers, and then return to his friends the next spring!'" (Seymour, p.41-45)

Kicking Bear's message had combined elements of tribal myth and Christianity to emphasize the destruction of the Americans, as well as a return to the traditional ways of life, and one of the men who listened to Kicking Bear's message was Little Wound, who returned to his people and gathered 300 of them to stage ghost dances of their own. However, Little Wound added a crucial wrinkle to Kicking Bear's message of an impending confrontation with the Americans by telling the crowd that weapons would not hurt any Lakota who used a "ghost shirt": "Wakan-tanka told me personally that the earth was now bad and worn out. He said we needed a new dwelling place where the rascally whites could not disturb us. So he instructed me to return to my people, the Lakotas, and tell them that if they would be constant in the dance, and pay no attention to the whites, he would shortly come to our aid. If the high priests would make medicine-shirts for the dancers and pray over them, no harm could come to the wearer. The bullets of any whites who tried to stop the ghost dance would fall to the ground without doing anyone harm, and the person who fired such shots would drop dead!"

The idea for the ghost shirts derived from holy shirts, which Native Americans believed warded off evil. Thus, in Little Wound's mind, if holy shirts warded off evil, then they must also ward off bullets, which he believed were a form of evil. For his part, Kicking Bear saw that the idea of the ghost shirt fit perfectly into his belief about Indians overcoming the technologies of the Americans, so he also began using the idea of ghost shirts. Ghost shirts would become standard for warriors, and ghost dresses for women dancers also became common. They were usually made of white muslin, which could be painted in the front and back with certain colors: blue on the back with a straight yellow line, which was accompanied by a picture or symbol of an eagle.

Chapter 3: Sitting Bull and the Ghost Dance

Sitting Bull

While the ghost dance picked up steam among the Lakota, the movement gained a renowned figure when Sitting Bull, unquestionably the most well-known member of the Lakota and perhaps the most famous Native American alive, became a proponent of the ghost dance. After hearing of the popularity of the ghost dance, he asked Kicking Bear to come to his village and tell them of his experiences with the messiah. By

By now, however, the U.S. Indian agents among the Lakota were becoming suspicious of the ghost dance and its message of conflict with whites. Agent James McLaughlin believed Sitting Bull was a threat, and the presence of Kicking Bear and Sitting Bull together brought him to action, as he sent a squad of Indian policemen to Sitting Bull, asking him to tell Kicking Bear to leave the area. However, when the policemen arrived in the middle of Kicking Bear's story of the messiah, they were overawed by it and did not follow their instructions to get Kicking Bear to leave.

McLaughlin

Angered by what transpired with his Indian police, McLaughlin sent one of his trusted officers, Chatka, to confront Kicking Bear. Chatka was able to get Kicking Bear and his men to leave the area and followed them all the way back into the Cheyenne reservation, but as soon as Kicking Bear left, Sitting Bull, who was deeply offended by the way the Indian police had forced out his guest, went into his cabin and returned with the peace pipe he had smoked with the white commander at Fort Buford when he had returned from Canada nearly a decade earlier. Facing the crowd that remained in the area, he spoke, "Do you see what I have here? It is my most sacred possession,. With it I pledged a life of peace to the white man. But the pledge is no longer any good because of the way the white man has betrayed us and humiliated us, and I will show you what I think of my life in the struggle now approaching..."

Sitting Bull then broke the pipe as the crowd cheered, and the ghost dance started up once more. Other acts of defiance against the Americans followed, and the Lakota interpreted them as being increasingly important in signaling the coming conflict between the Indians and the Americans. The first of these acts occurred at Pine Ridge when a new Indian agent, Daniel Royer, began pleading with the federal government for Army soldiers to take over control of the area. The Bureau of Indian Affairs, a civilian organization, refused to grant Royer's request, as it did not want to cede power to the military unless it was compelled to do so because of an outbreak of violence. Fortuitously for Royer, General Miles, came to Pine Ridge on other business, but in the process came into contact with ghost dancers at Medicine Root Creek. There he spoke with Little Wound, who announced to him:

> "My father, the great Chief Bear Coat...I am getting tired of hearing how all of us Indians ought to quit being Indians and start being white people; how we ought to do everything we are told, just because the white man tells us to. We are Indians, and we are not going to stop being Indians no matter what is done to us. Nor should we stop. We have a right to be what we are. We should behave like Indians and live like Indians.
>
> We can remain Indians by dancing the new ghost dance, and all of you chiefs here should go home and tell your people to dance it! As for my Oglalas, we intend to continue the ghost dance as long as we please. It matters little to us whether the white people like it or not..."

The second act of defiance occurred when Short Bull began insinuating that he now had some supernatural powers: "Now listen, my brothers! I have told you before that the day of judgment will come in two seasons. But we are getting so much interference from the whites that I am going to advance the time from what my Father above told me to do, so that the time will be shorter until the Indian is master again! Immediately, starting tomorrow, I am told by my Father above to start ghost-dancing on Pass Creek for one entire moon..." Pass Creek was farther west than Pine Ridge, and further away from the Indian agency. Short Bull knew that from there he could attract people from different villages to join him because he was now in a more central location.

One final act, this time a direct threat to Agent Royer, would lead to the entrance of the military into the Lakota reservation. During a ration day in which numerous Indian families were at the agency to get supplies, the Indian police under Lieutenant Thunder Bear attempted to arrest a Native American named Little, but during the process of the arrest, a crowd of Oglala warriors, almost all of whom were ghost dancers, circled the policemen as some members of the nearby crowd shouted "Kill them! Kill them! Let's burn down the agency!"

As things threatened to spiral out of control, a man named American Horse tried to calm the situation and prevent bloodshed: "Stop this! What do you think you are doing? Are you going to kill these men of our own race? What will happen then? Are you going to kill these helpless white men here and their women and children, also? And then what do you think will happen? What will these bold deeds of yours lead to? How long do you think you will be able to hold out? Your country here is surrounded with railroads, and thousands of white soldiers will be here within a few days. What ammunition do you have? What provisions do you have? What will become of your women and children when the soldiers attack? Think, think, my brothers! This is child's madness!"

The warriors ended up leaving with Little, and the Indian police were powerless to continue with his arrest. This event caused Agent Royer to send an urgent message to his superiors: "Indians are dancing in the snow and are wild and crazy. I have fully informed you that employees and government property are at the mercy of these dancers. Why delay by further investigation? We need protection and we need it now. The leaders should be arrested and confined in some military post until the matter is quieted, and this should be done at once."

With that, the Commissioner of Indian Affairs conceded that he had lost control of the situation and called for General John R. Brooke to send troops into the Pine Ridge and Rosebud reservations. Brooke would arrive three days later with 370 soldiers, and the arrival of the soldiers set off two movements of Indians on the reservations. Brooke sent messengers to the area's villages, telling "friendly" Indians to come to Pine Ridge so they could be protected by the soldiers. At the same time, Little Wound sent his own messengers, telling faithful ghost dancers to meet at the mouth of White Clay Creek, 20 miles to the northwest of Pine Ridge.

Brooke

As the military became aware of the gathering at White Clay Creek, they sent reinforcements to bolster the number of soldiers under Brooke's command. In all, by early December 1890, there were approximately 3,000 U.S. soldiers stationed in Lakota territory, and their intent was to crush the rebellious spirit of the Lakota once and for all. While Agent Royer was happy to have the army take control of the situation, McLaughlin still wanted to delay the arrival of troops onto his area so that he could arrest Sitting Bull. McLaughlin believed Sitting Bull was a leader of the rebellion among the Hunkpapa band, and he wanted Sitting Bull removed.

McLaughlin began by having his Indian police keep close watch on Sitting Bull, until it was decided that the arrest of Sitting Bull should take place on December 20th, when most of the area's Indians would be at the agency receiving supplies. McLaughlin's orders to Lieutenant Bull's Head included the message, "If he should [attempt to leave], you must stop him. If he does not listen to you, do as you see fit. Use your own discretion in the matter and it will be all right!"

However, McLaughlin was forced to change his plans when they discovered that Sitting Bull was preparing to leave the area: "Sitting Bull has received a letter from the Pine Ridge outfit asking him to come over there as God was about to appear. Sitting Bull's people want him to go, but he has sent a letter to you asking your permission, and if you do not give it he is going to go anyway. He has been fitting up his horses to stand a long ride, and will go horseback in case he is pursued. Bull Head would like to arrest him at once, before he has a chance of giving them the slip. He thinks that if Sitting Bull gets the start, it will be impossible to catch him."

While McLaughlin's Indian police moved into position to arrest Sitting Bull, a detachment of soldiers from Fort Yates arrived to back them up should the situation turn violent. Aiding the Indian police was the fact that a ghost dance had continued until early evening and everyone was exhausted. This enhanced the element of surprise, and just before dawn on December 15, the police surrounded Sitting Bull's cabin and Lieutenant Bull Head entered and ordered Sitting Bull out: "Come, father, I am ordered to take you into the agency." Sitting Bull, unsure of what was going on, seemed to be complying with the request.

As they began exiting the cabin, Sitting Bull's bodyguard, Catch-the-Bear, came on to the scene, where he came face-to-face with Bull Head, a man with whom he had a deep hatred from past conflicts. Meanwhile, Sitting Bull's son, Crow Foot, mocked his father for going with the police without resisting, and this caused Sitting Bull to struggle against his captors. As the scuffle continued, Catch-the-Bear moved alongside Bull Head, who had a hold of one of Sitting Bull's arms, and shot him in the side. As this occurred, the wounded Bull Head drew his own revolver and shot Sitting Bull. Red Tomahawk, another of the Indian police, also fired at Sitting Bull. Policeman Alone Man then pulled out his own gun and killed Catch-the-Bear.

The series of gunshots set off a confrontation between the policemen and the crowd of roughly 100 warriors that had descended on the scene. In the ensuing melee, the policemen managed to detach themselves and drag their wounded into one of the cabins, where they tried to hold out. Luckily, the troops from Fort Yates had heard the commotion and entered the village, forcing the crowd to disperse. The followers of Sitting Bull then fled into the woods, many leaving behind their belongings. While messengers were able to convince about 250 to return, 150 continued on toward the southwest.

All told, Sitting Bull, his son Crow Foot, and his adopted Assiniboine brother Jumping Bull were all killed, as were nine others. A number of Lakota policemen were also killed in the ensuing melee. Not surprisingly, many Native Americans view Sitting Bull's death as nothing less than an assassination, and a current movement still seeks to establish the day of his death (December 15) as a national holiday. They believe that because the government feared that he might join the Ghost Dancers and lead another Native American revolt, they ended his life, but either way, his death again demonstrated the misunderstandings so prevalent in relations between the U.S. and Native Americans.

1891 newspaper illustration of a Ghost Dance

Chapter 4: Big Foot and the Stronghold

"The difficult Indian problem cannot be solved permanently at this end of the line. It requires the fulfillment of Congress of the treaty obligations that the Indians were entreated and coerced into signing. They signed away a valuable portion of their reservation, and it is now occupied by white people, for which they have received nothing. They understood that ample provision would be made for their support; instead, their supplies have been reduced, and much of the time they have been living on half and two-thirds rations. Their crops, as well as the crops of the white people, for two years have been almost total failures. The dissatisfaction is wide spread, especially among the Sioux, while the Cheyennes have been on the verge of starvation, and were forced to commit depredations to sustain life. These facts are beyond question, and the evidence is positive and sustained by thousands of witnesses." – General Nelson Miles in a telegram to Washington, D.C. on December 19, 1890

The Lakota who left to start ghost dance camps were unsuccessful at sustaining these endeavors. Little Wound, for example, whose camp at White Clay contained roughly 2,000 Indians, soon found that the logistics of coordinating them was too much to handle, and within a week, he returned to the agency with his followers. Big Road and No Water, along with their followers, also quickly returned to the agency. The other major camp, created by Short Bull and Kicking Bear and containing a large number of ghost dancers, also experienced enough problems that the leaders feared the breakup of the community into bands that would drift back to the agency. Ultimately, Short Bull decided that the best course of action was to march to White Clay to join up with Little Wound.

The march took a week to complete, and upon arriving at White Clay, Short Bull and Kicking Bear found that Little Wound, No Water, and Big Road had all returned to the agency. This was a huge blow for Short Bull and Kicking Bear, who also learned that the number of soldiers on the reservation had been bolstered by reinforcements, including Custer's old unit, the 7th Cavalry. The Native American leaders understandably feared the 7th cavalry would probably be looking for revenge after Little Big Horn, which had occurred 14 years earlier, so Short Bull and Kicking Bear decided that the best course of action was to move as far away from the soldiers as possible. They eventually settled on an area called the Stronghold, a plateau with only a series of narrow paths leading up to it. As Short Bull stated, "Now, my brothers, I am thinking of that point, that island, at the north side of the big table -- it is part of the big table only it is not part of it. If we were on top of that point, we would not even have to defend the sharp saddle connecting it with the larger table, because no man can cross it. We would need only to defend the two or three steep deer trails up its sides. The bluecoats could never get their horses and guns up those trails if we were defending them."

Short Bull and Kicking Bear believed they would be safe on top of the Stronghold, and they began planning their journey to that location. As the ghost dancers were gathering supplies and readying themselves for the march to the Stronghold, Short Bull also sent messengers to Wounded Knee Creek, where Two Strike led a group of ghost dancers. Short Bull instructed Two Strike to meet them at the Stronghold, and Two Strike agreed to the request.

When General John R. Brooke began receiving word of the Indians' movement to the Stronghold, he asked Father John Jutz, a missionary trusted by the natives, if he would travel to the Stronghold and speak to them. Jutz agreed, and as he heard the grievances of the leaders, he learned about the sense of betrayal that the Native Americans felt at their treatment by the federal government. Once Jutz had heard all of their complaints, he attempted to convince them to come back to the agency: "My friends, it is getting light in the East. I know there is much justice on your side. I can only beg you not to stop listening to what the soldier chief wants to say to you. If you would only pick a few to go back with me, I myself, whom you trust, will guarantee your safety. I want you to talk to General Brooke. He is an honorable man. I will send word ahead that you must come with completely free passage in and out of the agency."

The leaders at the Stronghold sent a delegation to meet with Brooke, where they reiterated their stance on their relationship with the Americans. Brooke argued that they could settle their grievances once they left the Stronghold and returned to the agency, and although no decision was made as to whether they should return or remain at the Stronghold, a sense of doubt did begin to creep into the minds of the delegation about continuing their rebellion.

The debate on whether to remain or return to the agency continued once the delegation returned to the Stronghold and informed the leadership of what had occurred in their meeting with General Brooke. After deliberating for a number of days, Two Strike, on the afternoon of December 10th, stood up and announced that he was returning to the agency. Crow Dog quickly stood up and voiced his agreement with Two Strike, which set off an argument between those who wanted to leave and those who wished to remain. The fighting only stopped when everyone noticed Crow Dog, who had pulled his blanket over his head in shame: "Is it fitting that brothers in the Lakota family should kill each other? I myself am going to White Clay [the agency]. Kill me if you want to, right now, and prevent me from starting. I believe the agent's words are true, and it is better to return than to stay here any longer."

The faction that wished to stay at the Stronghold acknowledged that they had been defeated, and by the end of the day, most of the camp had been packed up and a train of Native Americans were slowly making their way down the narrow paths leading down to the canyon's floor. For all intents and purposes, their rebellion had ended.

Meanwhile, as the arguments at the Stronghold were taking place, one of the ghost dance's main proponents, Big Foot (also known as Spotted Elk), had returned to his village at Deep Creek. Big Foot was summoned to meet with Colonel Sumner, who wanted to get a picture of his intentions, and Big Foot declared that he did not want to become involved with the rebellion: "We have no intention of leaving our homes here, where we are comfortable. But I have to tell you something honestly: We do not get nearly enough rations from the agency to keep us in good health. The young mothers are poorly fed and as a result they have no milk in their breasts for their babies. The children too often get sick and die. If our young warriors are nervous and angry, it is because their families are hungry and they do not get enough clothing to keep them warm through the hard winter."

After meeting with Big Foot, Sumner believed that he was building a strong relationship with the leader, and he reported to his superiors that he had the situation under control: "I have held a council with all the principal chiefs in this section of the country, and find that they are peaceably disposed and inclined to obey orders; but from their talk, as well as from reports I have received from officers here and others, I believe they are really hungry and suffering from want of clothing and covering. I advise that 1,000 rations be sent me at once for issue to them, and authority to purchase a certain amount of fresh beef." (Seymour, p.105)

During this time of meeting with Sumner, Big Foot received messages from Red Cloud's agency that they needed his help in meeting with the Oglala to "make a peace." They hoped that Big Foot's presence would help them convince Kicking Bear, Big Foot's protégé, to relent on his attempts to continue holding out. However, Big Foot saw the dangers that could come from going to Red Cloud, especially in entangling his band in the issue of the developing rebellion, so in an attempt to postpone a decision, Big Foot decided the best course of action was to take his entire band to the Cheyenne River agency for the next issuance of their supplies, which would occur on December 22nd.

As Big Foot and his band began traveling toward the agency at Fort Bennett, Colonel Sumner received orders from his superiors to arrest Big Foot. Due to Sitting Bull's death while in the custody of Indian police, and also due to the fact that Kicking Bear and Short Bull were out of reach at the Stronghold, it had been decided that Big Foot, who had been listed as a "dangerous ghost-dance fanatic", was now the army's top priority. This was an embarrassing moment for Sumner, who had let Big Foot leave the area unsupervised only to discover that this man had now been categorized as a criminal, and naturally, Big Foot was unaware of the orders for his arrest. Big Foot eventually received word from scouts that a large detachment of soldiers from Fort Sully along the Missouri River were making their way directly toward him, and believing that he could not make his way to the agency with the soldiers coming toward them, he decided that the best course of action was to return to his village.

For Colonel Sumner, reports were filtering in that some of Sitting Bull's Hunkpapa Sioux had taken flight after his death and were moving toward Big Foot. Sumner believed that if they were allowed to join together, they might turn violent, so in an effort to stop this from occurring, Sumner sent his cavalry out after Big Foot. In fact, a small group of Sitting Bull's Hunkpapas had run into Big Foot's band and had joined up with them, but even after he had learned of Sitting Bull's death, this did not mean that Big Foot was going to turn violent. Nevertheless, Big Foot was now trapped between two forces; the soldiers from Fort Sully had stopped him from getting to Fort Bennett, and now Sumner's cavalry were blocking his path back to his village. Big Foot decided that he needed to speak to Sumner, and in their subsequent meeting, Big Foot reiterated that he meant to travel to the agency at Fort Bennett, but that he would follow Sumner's orders whatever they might be.

Sumner told Big Foot that he was not allowed to travel to Fort Bennett, but he led Big Foot to believe that he would be returning to his village with Sumner's cavalry as an escort, when in fact he was going to be led past his village and on to Fort Meade, where he would be arrested. Hints of the violence to come occurred the next day when two wagons got jammed together. The cavalrymen riding alongside the Indians' wagons began to curse at the wagon drivers, which caused Black Fox, Big Foot's son-in-law, to become enraged. He shouted, "I don't care to have my relatives abused this way by any white man!" and raised his rifle at the nearest cavalryman. Potential violence was averted when the wagons were untangled and began moving again, and after Big Foot arrived to calm things down.

As they arrived back at Big Foot's village, Sumner was left with a dilemma. He understood that many of the warriors among Big Foot's band were on edge, and that forcing them to continue past their village could bring on violence. As he was debating what to do, Big Foot rode up to him and asked for his people to be allowed to return to their cabins. He offered to go with Sumner to the military camp, but he asked for the women and children, many of whom were cold and tired, to be allowed to return to their homes for the evening. Sumner agreed to allow Big Foot's band to return to their homes on the condition that Big Foot come to the military camp with Sitting Bull's Hunkpapas the following morning.

Later that night, Sumner received a dispatch from General Miles, who had personally come to Rapid City in the Black Hills to take charge of the campaign against the Lakota. He asked that Sumner "push on rapidly to Meade with your prisoners, be careful they do not escape, and look out for other Indians." Sumner wrote back, telling Miles of the plan for Big Foot to come to the military camp the next day, but when Big Foot failed to arrive, Sumner was forced to decide on a course of action. He believed that to enter the village and arrest Big Foot by force would lead to a battle between his cavalrymen and Big Foot's warriors, which would no doubt be costly and violent, so he instead decided it was best to get Big Foot to go to Fort Bennett, where the army officers there could arrest him.

When Sumner sent scouts down to the village to see what was going on, they discovered that, at some point the previous night, Sitting Bull's Hunkpapas had been tipped off that Sumner wanted them at the military camp. The Hunkpapas had secretly left, while Big Foot, who was embarrassed at this turn of events since he had given Sumner his word, sent out his own scouts to try to find them and bring them back. Sumner enlisted the help of a neighboring rancher named John Dunn, who spoke to Big Foot at his cabin and informed him that he was supposed to go to Fort Bennett. Big Foot was now angered that he had been forbidden to go to Fort Bennett and was now being asked to go there. He complained to Dunn, "If he wants us to go to Bennett, why did he not send us there when he met us at Cherry Creek, two days ago? Why has he hauled us all the way back here, only to tell us now to start out again immediately on that long march eastward? I do not understand such nonsense."

After Dunn calmed Big Foot down, he agreed to go to Fort Bennett the next day, as "we do not want a fight." Once Dunn had left, however, Big Foot convened a meeting among his band: "My brothers, I am much troubled by what is going on here. First I was headed for Fort Bennett to get our rations and they came and got us and brought us back here merely because we were trying to help our Hunkpapa relatives. Now I am told that I must start again for Bennett tomorrow morning or the soldiers will come in and shoot us and arrest us. We know and they know that there are many soldiers coming toward us on the Cheyenne, and now we are to be drive straight into their midst. What is the meaning of all this?"

In the ensuing debate, some wanted to go to the agency once more, avoiding the troops along the Cheyenne River, and others wanted to head for Pine Ridge to accept the offer of Red Cloud to help make peace among the rebellious ghost dancers. However, Big Foot decided to choose a different path, announcing, "Let us break camp and move up into the hills to the south until we find out exactly what the white soldier chief intends. If everything is quiet we can come back down here in the morning, or we can start east to Bennett. Meanwhile our women and children will be out in the open and able to get away from the shooting if there is any trouble. This is my home. This is my place. If they want to come here and kill me, let them come. I have done no wrong to the white people. My heart is bitter about the threat to shoot us. What have we done except obey the soldier chief?"

As Big Foot and his band packed up to leave their village, Sumner's scouts, who had been watching from a distance, tried to make sense of what was going on. Were they leaving for Fort Bennett as quickly as possible? Were they going somewhere else altogether? A scout named Charging First returned to Sumner's camp at twilight and reported on what was going on, telling the camp that Big Foot's women and children were acting as if a fight was coming on. At the same time, they were packing in a way that signaled that they would be traveling quickly and over rough country.

After hearing the report, Sumner decided to move his cavalry closer to Big Foot's village, but he miscalculated the speed with which Big Foot and his people were moving. The entire village had made it eight miles up Deep Creek before Sumner realized that they had left, and when they stopped for a short rest, Big Foot called his council together to figure out their next move. The council issued an ultimatum to their chief: they wanted to go to Pine Ridge to take up Red Cloud's offer. They did not want to risk being caught between two groups of soldiers, and they were very worried by Sumner's maneuvering of the previous few days. Big Foot, who by this time was quite ill, decided not to oppose his council and instead allowed them to continue on toward Pine Ridge.

When Sumner's scouts finally found Big Foot's band and returned to notify Sumner of their findings, they had gotten 25 miles away and it would be very difficult for Sumner's men to overtake them. At the same time, Sumner received another set of orders from General Miles: "The attitude of Big Foot has been defiant and hostile and you are authorized to arrest him or any of his people and to take him to Meade or Bennett...The division commander directs, therefore, that you secure Big Foot and the Cheyenne River Indians, and the Standing Rock Indians, and if necessary round up the whole camp and disarm them, and take them to Meade or Bennett." Sumner had to tell Miles that he had lost contact with Big Foot, and that Big Foot's group had made their way out of his jurisdiction.

Big Foot's band made their way forward, stopping only occasionally and only for short periods of time to rest. In just over a day, Big Foot's band of 300 people had marched nearly 60 miles, and Big Foot had thoroughly confused the army officers attempting to track him. The military was attempting to stop a rebellion that was centered on White Clay and the Stronghold, but Big Foot was not attempting to bolster the ranks of the rebels; instead, he was trying to get away from any potential fighting and lead his people to safety. But even though Big Foot was not attempting to join the rebels, his decision to attempt to start moving away signaled to the military that he was actually rebelling and a potentially dangerous man who needed to be found and stopped at any cost.

The military's inability to understand that Big Foot's people were not in a state of rebellion was apparent when Colonel Carr was called on to help Sumner and sweep the areas near the Stronghold to stop them from potentially joining the rebels stationed there. When Big Foot's people stopped to rest on the White River, one of Carr's units was camping just 10 miles away, but they did not discover Big Foot's band because they were so caught up with the idea that Big Foot wanted to reach the Stronghold that they were only focusing on those areas.

On the morning of the 25th of December, Big Foot sent messengers ahead to Pine Ridge to advise the Native Americans there that he would be arriving shortly, but when the messengers returned, they told Big Foot that once they had announced his impending arrival, a detachment of soldiers had moved out from Pine Ridge as far as the Wounded Knee trading post and were now stationed there. These soldiers were directly in their path, thus blocking their way to Pine Ridge. As the council debated what to do, they were approached by an Oglala named Shaggy Feather, who had been sent by the Oglala leaders to tell Big Foot that the Stronghold rebels had given up and would be returning to Pine Ridge in two days. They asked Big Foot to delay his arrival so that they would all arrive together in a show of force, but Big Foot, whose illness had progressed into pneumonia, believed he was too sick to delay for two days. He fatefully decided that the best course of action was to make contact with the soldiers at Wounded Knee, tell them that they came in peace, and then make their way to Pine Ridge with them.

Chapter 5: The Massacre

"The Pioneer has before declared that our only safety depends upon the total extermination of the Indians. Having wronged them for centuries, we had better, in order to protect our civilization, follow it up by one more wrong and wipe these untamed and untamable creatures from the face of the earth. In this lies future safety for our settlers and the soldiers who are under incompetent commands. Otherwise, we may expect future years to be as full of trouble with the redskins as those have been in the past..". – L. Frank Baum (author of *The Wonderful Wizard of Oz*), writing for the *Aberdeen Saturday Pioneer*, January 3, 1891.

Upon the surrender of Short Bull and Kicking Bear's camp at the Stronghold, Big Foot's band was now considered the only remaining "hostiles" out in the field, and the orders that filtered down the chain of command from General Miles clearly indicated he believed Big Foot's band was dangerous. The orders also demonstrated that he was willing to use force to subdue them: "I have directed the troops to ride down and capture or destroy the few that have escaped from Standing Rock. General Brooke has more than 1,000 lodges or 5,000 Indians under his control at Pine Ridge, but there are still 50 lodges or over 200 fighting men in the Bad Lands that are very defiant and hostile."

In further dispatches to his subordinates, Miles wrote on the 26th, "Big Foot is cunning and his Indians are very bad..." On the 27th, Brooke's aide relayed the message to his men: "I am directed by the Commanding General to say that he thinks Big Foot's party must be in front of you somewhere...Find his trail and follow, or find his hiding place and capture him. If he fights, destroy him." Finally, on December 28th, Miles wrote to Brooke, "Use force enough!" (Seymour, p.147)

With that, Major Samuel Whitside was ordered out from Pine Ridge at the head of four units from the 7th Cavalry, as well as a platoon of artillery and two Hotchkiss cannons. He went directly to Wounded Knee Creek, where he set up headquarters at the residence of Louis Mousseau, the Wounded Knee storekeeper. Whitside quickly sent out scouts to make contact with Big Foot's band, but they were unable to find them.

Whitside

The next day, December 28, Big Foot's advance riders happened upon some of Whitside's scouts, and as soon as news of contact reached the camp, Whitside ordered his men forward. Whitside ordered his men to form skirmish lines and set up his Hotchkiss cannons at the front of the formation, so as Big Foot approached, he tied a white cloth to a long pole and attached it to his wagon, calling for a peaceful meeting. As Whitside met with Big Foot, they began discussing what was going on. On seeing the condition of Big Foot, who was suffering heavily from the combination of pneumonia and frenetic travel, Whitside asked through his interpreter, "Are you able to talk?" When Big Foot replied that he could, Whitside stated, "I heard that you came out of Cheyenne River as a war party, and I've been looking for you. Where are you going?" Big Foot replied. "I want to see my people on White Clay Creek, so I'm going to the agency." When Whitside asked why he was going there, Big Foot replied, "Because they sent for me. They want me to make peace and I will get a hundred horses." Whitside accepted this answer, telling the chief, "All right, but I want you to come on into Wounded Knee and camp there."

Big Foot accepted this, and everything seemed to be going smoothly until Whitside remembered that he had been ordered to disarm the band. Whitside turned to his interpreter and said, "John, I want their horses and guns!" John Shangreau, the interpreter, told Whitside, "If you do that you're liable to have a fight right here, and if that happens you'll kill all these women and children while the men get away from us!" Whitside was unsure of what to do, but in the end he decided that they would take Big Foot and his band to the camp first and then disarm them there. After making his decision, Whitside quickly sent off a message to General Brooke letting him know that Big Foot's band had been captured. Whitside also asked that Colonel James W. Forsyth and the rest of the 7th Cavalry be sent to Wounded Knee to help in disarming the Indians. General Brooke agreed to this and quickly sent Forsyth and his men out.

Forsyth

Meanwhile, Big Foot and his band set up camp along a ravine bordering Whitside's camp, and they agreed to have their horses staked out away from the camp. Colonel Forsyth arrived later that night and set up camp on the opposite end from Big Foot. With the added presence of Forsythe's men, there were now 500 white soldiers and Indian army scouts surrounding Big Foot's band of 200 women, children, and elderly, along with about 100 young men of fighting age. The goal, as Whitside and Forsyth saw it, was to put up such a strong show of force that Big Foot and his warriors would accept being disarmed without putting up resistance.

On the morning of December 29, an elder named Horn Cloud called a meeting among some of the warriors and told them, "I have to tell you truthfully that I do not much like the looks of things here, my sons, and I want to give you some advice. If any of our brothers try to start trouble, do not join in with them. Of course if the white soldiers start shooting, you will do whatever you have to do. In that case, my dear sons, stand together soberly in front of your old folks and little ones, protecting them as long as you can. And if any of you die in this fashion I will be satisfied. But let us not get panicky, whatever happens. If one or two of our men start trouble, they will be arrested and put in jail, and I do not want any of my sons to get into such a useless mess. So stay calm -- unless we should be attacked by soldiers. Then you must defend yourselves and all of us."

Meanwhile, Forsyth and Whitside were making final preparations for disarming the band, and Forsyth told his subordinates, "Now, gentlemen, getting their guns away from these bucks may be a little touchy, and I want it perfectly understood what our orders are. We are going to disarm these Indians, and we are ordered to prevent the escape of any of them. If they fight, we are to destroy them. Big Foot's bunch have made fools of us long enough, and I don't intend to let them get away with it here. If there is any firing on their part, I want your men to shoot. Is that clear?"

Once the soldiers were properly set up to receive and disarm the Native Americans, Forsyth addressed Big Foot's band: "I want to assure you Minneconjous that you and your people are perfectly safe under the protection of your older friends, the soldiers. All of your troubles are coming to an end. We will not let you starve any more, but will feed you well. However, in order to be sure there is no trouble of any kind, I must ask you to turn in your guns to me, and then we will go along to the agency." This announcement was met with anger from many of the warriors, and High Hawk and another headman went to Big Foot's tent seeking advice on how to proceed. Big Foot, who was most likely in a state of confusion due to illness, told them, " This is the third time they have tried to take the guns away from us. I'll tell you what: You give them the bad guns and keep the good ones!"

When Forsyth learned of what Big Foot had said, he approached the chief himself and told the interpreter, "Tell the chief that I want him to tell the men to surrender their guns." Big Foot responded to the interpreter that they had surrendered their guns already at the Cheyenne agency. At this point, Forsyth became furious: "You tell Big Foot he claims his Indians have no guns, yet yesterday at the time of their surrender they were all well armed! He is plainly deceiving me. Tell him he needn't have any fear about giving up the arms, because I wish to treat him with nothing but kindness." When Big Foot did not respond, Forsyth ordered his men to begin collecting their weapons.

At this point, a medicine man named Yellow Bird began dancing and praying. He then scooped up a handful of soil, raised his arms aloft, and let the dirt drift away in the breeze, telling the band, "Warriors! Do not be afraid! Let your hearts be strong to meet the test that is now before you. There are soldiers all about us and they have lots of bullets. But I have received assurances that their bullets cannot penetrate us! The prairie is large, and the bullets will go over you into the prairie! Just as you saw my dust drift away, so will the bullets drift away harmlessly!" Not surprisingly, when Forsyth's interpreter relayed what Yellow Bird had said, the soldiers began to get nervous. It seemed the situation was quickly spiraling out of control and increasing the likelihood of a violent confrontation.

Forsyth ordered his men to continue disarming the Lakota, but when they tried to take the rifle of a warrior named Black Coyote, he became agitated. As two soldiers wrestled with him over the rifle, the gun went off, after which the soldiers immediately began firing into the gathering. Big Foot and many members of his council were killed in the first volleys, but some warriors who still had possession of their guns began firing back and those without guns charged the soldiers. As the women and children who were still at the camp began running, they too became targets. In addition to the rifle fire coming from the soldiers, the Hotchkiss cannons that had been mounted on the high ground overlooking Big Foot's camp began to rain bullets down on the crowd, killing and wounding Native Americans and fellow soldiers alike.

The hill where the Hotchkiss cannons were positioned

Big Foot's corpse at Wounded Knee

While the confusion of the first gun going off can be credited with leading to the initial volley, eyewitness accounts made clear that the soldiers became unhinged. Captain Edward S. Godfrey, a member of the 7th Cavalry who had been at Little Bighorn and was at Wounded Knee, later described the "fight": "I know the men did not aim deliberately and they were greatly excited. I don't believe they saw their sights. They fired rapidly but it seemed to me only a few seconds till there was not a living thing before us; warriors, squaws, children, ponies, and dogs ... went down before that unaimed fire."

Naturally, some of the men, along with the women and children, started attempting to escape the slaughter, as one survivor explained: "many Indians broke into the ravine; some ran up the ravine and to favorable positions for defense." However, it was mostly to no avail. As Hugh McGinnis of the 7th Cavalry noted, ""General Nelson A. Miles who visited the scene of carnage, following a three day blizzard, estimated that around 300 snow shrouded forms were strewn over the countryside. He also discovered to his horror that helpless children and women with babes in their arms had been chased as far as two miles from the original scene of encounter and cut down without mercy by the troopers. ... Judging by the slaughter on the battlefield it was suggested that the soldiers simply went berserk. For who could explain such a merciless disregard for life? ...

As I see it the battle was more or less a matter of spontaneous combustion, sparked by mutual distrust." American Horse, a survivor at Wounded Knee, similarly described the scene: "There was a woman with an infant in her arms who was killed as she almost touched the flag of truce ... A mother was shot down with her infant; the child not knowing that its mother was dead was still nursing ... The women as they were fleeing with their babies were killed together, shot right through ... and after most all of them had been killed a cry was made that all those who were not killed or wounded should come forth and they would be safe. Little boys ... came out of their places of refuge, and as soon as they came in sight a number of soldiers surrounded them and butchered them there."

Chapter 6: The Aftermath

"This monument is erected by surviving relatives and other Ogalala and Cheyenne River Sioux Indians in memory of the Chief Big Foot massacre December 29, 1890. Col. Forsyth in command of US troops. Big Foot was a great chief of the Sioux Indians. He often said, 'I will stand in peace till my last day comes.' He did many good and brave deeds for the white man and the red man. Many innocent women and children who knew no wrong died here." – Memorial placed at Wounded Knee

Some of the carnage at Wounded Knee

A burial party preparing to bury some of the dead

Some frozen bodies remained unburied weeks later.

When the shooting stopped about an hour after the first gun had gone off, an estimated 150-300 Native Americans had been killed, some of whom were killed miles away from the initial fighting. 25 soldiers were dead and dozens were wounded as well, mostly due to friendly fire. The few surviving Native Americans were herded to Pine Ridge, but there were plenty of dead to bury and wounded to treat. Elaine Goodale, a teacher living nearby whose school was converted into a makeshift hospital, later recalled, "Our patients cried and moaned incessantly, and every night some dead were carried out. In spite of all we could do, most of the injuries proved fatal. The few survivors were heartbroken and apathetic, for nearly all their men had been killed on the spot." (Di Silvestro, p.89)

A picture of the survivors of Wounded Knee with the caption "What's Left of Big Foot's band".

When Miles came to Wounded Knee a few days after the fighting, he was so disgusted at what had happened that he immediately attempted to remove Forsyth from command. However, after an investigation, the Secretary of War eventually reinstated Forsyth, and members of the 7th Cavalry went about trying to raise money to erect a memorial on the field to their fallen comrades. Relatives of the Native Americans at Wounded Knee erected their own memorial in 1903 as well.

In a further stamp of approval, the government eventually awarded 20 medals of honor to soldiers at Wounded Knee. On top of that, some of the medals were awarded to soldiers who had chased fleeing Indians, such as this citation: "SULLIVAN, THOMAS Rank and organization: Private, Company E, 7th U.S. Cavalry. Place and date: At Wounded Knee Creek, S. Dak., 29 December 1890. Entered service at: Newark, N.J. Birth: Ireland. Date of issue: 17 December 1891. Citation: Conspicuous bravery in action against Indians concealed in a ravine." As one Lakota, William Thunder Hawk, later complained, "The Medal of Honor is meant to reward soldiers who act heroically. But at Wounded Knee, they didn't show heroism; they showed cruelty."

A picture of General Miles at Wounded Knee

In general, the American public was pleased with the results, and for American newspapers covering the incident, many published stories like the one in the *Chadron Democrat* on January 1, 1891, which praised the action and predicted with sarcastic scorn that politicians would ultimately punish the military officers for their success: "For once it has occurred that more Indians than soldiers have been slain, and we doubt not but that either Gen. Miles or Brooke will be cashiered from the service as was Gen. Harney for such pitiless bloodshed. Nothing will be done about the poor soldiers who were slain, but the Indian department is undoubtedly already getting in its work upon some crank of a congressman to present a bill before the august and wise body to investigate the cause that led to the late massacre and uncalled for slaughter of such dear, good Indians...we glory in the revenge of the Seventh, although they sustained a heavy loss, and notwithstanding there may have been but a few in the late fight left who belonged to the Seventh during Custer's life...We predict that the killing of Big Foot and his warriors will have a telling effect on the messiah craze, and will civilize more reds who are yet alive than all the power of God and education that has been pumped into them for the past 16 years." (Di Silvestro, p.92)

That prediction seemingly came true. According to Black Elk, a young warrior at the time of the Wounded Knee, the massacre killed the ghost dance: "And so it was all over. I did not know then how much was ended. When I look back now from this high hill of my old age, I can still see the butchered women and children lying heaped and scattered all along the crooked gulch as plain as when I saw them with eyes still young. And I can see that something else died there in the bloody mud, and was buried in the blizzard: A people's dream died there. It was a beautiful dream." (Di Silvestro, p.92) Indeed, when news spread about the events at Wounded Knee, it became clear to its adherents that the Ghost Dance had failed to live up to its promises. The decorated buckskin Ghost Dance shirts had failed to stop bullets, and, more disappointingly, the dead warriors and the buffalo had failed to return. Since the predictions of Wovoka (the original Ghost Dance prophet) proved false, the practice quickly disappeared, though some remained faithful to its outlandish claims. Isolated pockets of believers continued to carry on a version of the faith, but it was greatly diminished in terms of promising a return of the traditional plains horse culture. Shoshone Ghost Dancers performed the last known examples of the Ghost Dance rituals during the 1950s.

Bibliography

Andersson, Rani-Henrik. The Lakota Ghost Dance of 1890, University of Nebraska Press, 2009.

Brown, Dee. Bury My Heart at Wounded Knee: An Indian History of the American West, Owl Books (1970).

Coleman, William S.E. Voices of Wounded Knee, University of Nebraska Press (2000).

Di Silvestro, Roger. *In the Shadow of Wounded Knee: The Untold Final Chapter of the Indian Wars*. New York: Walker & Co., 2005.

Seymour, Forrest. *Sitanka: The Full Story of Wounded Knee*. W. Hanover, Massachusetts: The Christopher Publishing House, 1981.

Smith, Rex Alan. Moon of Popping Trees, University of Nebraska Press (1981).

Utley, Robert M. Last Days of the Sioux Nation, Yale University Press (1963).

Utley, Robert M. The Indian Frontier 1846–1890, University of New Mexico Press (2003).

Utley, Robert M. Frontier Regulars The United States Army and the Indian 1866–1891, MacMillan Publishing (1973).

Yenne, Bill. Indian Wars: The Campaign for the American West, Westholme (2005).

Champlin, Tim. A Trail To Wounded Knee : A Western Story, Five Star (2001).